Illustrated Daniel in Greek

GlossaHouse Illustrated Biblical Texts

Illustrated Daniel in Greek
GlossaHouse Illustrated Biblical Texts

T. Michael W. Halcomb   Andrew T. Keenan

GlossaHouse
Wilmore, KY
www.GlossaHouse.com

Illustrated Daniel in Greek: GlossaHouse Illustrated Biblical Texts
Copyright © 2019 by GlossaHouse, LLC

All rights reserved. No part of this work may be reproduced or transmitted in any form or by any means, electronic or mechanical, including photocopying and recording, or by means of any information storage or retrieval system, except as may be expressly permitted by the 1976 Copyright Act or in writing from the publisher. Requests for permission should be addressed in writing to the following:

GlossaHouse, LLC
110 Callis Circle
Wilmore, KY 40390

Bible. Daniel. Greek. 2019.
    Daniel : GlossaHouse illustrated Biblical Texts / T. Michael W. Halcomb, Andrew T. Keenan. – Wilmore, KY : GlossaHouse, [©2019].
    x, 35 pages : color illustrations ; 28 cm. – (Accessible Greek resources and online studies series. GlossaHouse Illustrated Biblical Texts. Bible)

Summary: The Greek text of Daniel is set within colorful illustrations to represent narration, dialogue, monologue, and scripture quotations, together with a new English version by GlossaHouse translators. Text in English and Koinē Greek.

ISBN: 9781942697916 (paperback)
Library of Congress Control Number: 2019952436.

    1. Bible. Daniel – Cartoons and comics.   I. Halcomb, T. Michael W. II. Keenan, Andrew T., III. LXX Septuagint (Rahlfs-Hanhart, 2nd ed.) VI. Title. V. Series. VI. Bible. Daniel. English. 2019.

The text of the LXX is from *Septuaginta*, edited by Alfred Rahlfs, Second, Revised Edition, edited by Robert Hanhart, © 2006 Deutsche Bibelgesellschaft, Stuttgart. Used by permission.

The English translation of Daniel LXX used here, the GlossaHouse English Version (GEV), is original and has been created by T. Michael W. Halcomb and Andrew T. Keenan.

The fonts used to create this work are available from linguistsoftware.com/lgku.htm.
Illustrations and general illustration layout Copyright © 2006 Neely Publishing LLC.
Cover Design by T. Michael W. Halcomb and Andrew T. Keenan
Book Design by T. Michael W. Halcomb, Andrew T. Keenan, and Fredrick J. Long
Illustration Design by Keith Neely

*Dedicated to those aspiring
to love and master Koine Greek*

AGROS

Accessible Greek Resources and Online Studies

SERIES EDITORS

T. Michael W. Halcomb   Fredrick J. Long

AGROS

The Greek word ἀγρός is a field where seeds are planted and growth occurs. It can also denote a small village or community that forms around such a field. The type of community envisioned here is one that attends to Holy Scripture, particularly one that encourages the use of biblical Greek. Accessible Greek Resources and Online Studies (AGROS) is a tiered curriculum suite featuring innovative readers, grammars, specialized studies, and other exegetical resources to encourage and foster the exegetical use of biblical Greek. The goal of AGROS is to facilitate the creation and publication of innovative and affordable print and digital resources for the exposition of Scripture within the context of the global church. The AGROS curriculum includes five tiers, and each tier is indicated on the book's cover: Tier 1 (Beginning I), Tier 2 (Beginning II), Tier 3 (Intermediate I), Tier 4 (Intermediate II), and Tier 5 (Advanced). There are also two resource tracks: Conversational and Translational. Both involve intensive study of morphology, grammar, syntax, and discourse features. The conversational track specifically values the spoken word, and the enhanced learning associated with speaking a language in actual conversation. The translational track values the written word, and encourages analytical study to aide in understanding and translating biblical Greek and other Greek literature. The two resource tracks complement one another and can be pursued independently or together.

Table of Contents

Introduction — xi-xix

ΔΑΝΙΗΛ (DANIEL)

Κεφ. Α´ (Ch. 1)	1-5
Κεφ. Β´ (Ch. 2)	5-9
Κεφ. Γ´ (Ch. 3)	9-13
Κεφ. Δ´ (Ch. 4)	13-17
Κεφ. Ε´ (Ch. 5)	17-21
Κεφ. F´ (Ch. 6)	21-28
Κεφ. Z´ (Ch. 7)	28-32
Κεφ. H´ (Ch. 8)	32-35
Κεφ. Θ´ (Ch. 9)	35-40
Κεφ. I´ (Ch. 10)	40-45
Κεφ. IA´ (Ch. 11)	45-49
Κεφ. IB´ (Ch. 12)	49-53

Introduction

The textual history of Daniel is quite messy. This is especially true when working with its Greek renditions. This also means that, in some ways, Daniel is quite controversial. We suspect that this volume, in its own ways, may add to the controversy. This is the case because the "final form" of our text, which mainly follows the Old Greek (OG) tradition, occasionally looks to the Theodotian (TH), Hebrew Masoretic (MT), and Latin Vulgate (VUL) traditions for insights. The end-result is overwhelmingly OG in nature but has a hint of TH mixed in. (See the chart on the following page for more details.) At the same time, there were instances where we felt it necessary to part ways with the OG or TH traditions and offer insights on items such as capitalization, punctuation, and versification (i.e. verse numbering). On the next few pages we list those differences and provide the principles of our method of translation.

Versification: At 3:23, for instance, the OG splits from TH. What we've chosen to do is follow the Protestant tradition in terms of versification but map the corresponding OG text to those verses when possible. Thus, we follow the versification of the NIV and KJV. This, however, does not mean we follow these texts in their translation choices. That is, where the NIV and KJV tend to follow the MT, which is often closer to TH, we tend to follow the OG. Because the OG is our main base text, we choose to work with it whenever possible while, at the same time, following versification that tends to follow Protestantism. The chart below helps visualize and make sense of how we've structured our final text.

For Dan 3:25-30, for example, we use the OG text, whose verse numbers are 3:92-97. When we follow the NIV and KJV texts for 4:1-3, we also use the Greek of TH. We do the same at 4:6-7, 4:33, and 4:37. We also leave out both 4:17a and 4:33a-b from OG. Concerning the 5:1 Intro, we follow Protestant tradition and omit that from our text altogether. In Dan 5, it should be noted that in the OG, despite the following verse numbers being omitted, will still follow this order: 14, 15, 18, 19, 20, 21, 22, 24, and 25. We also follow Protestant tradition in versification and, as a result, map 5:31-6:28 to the OG text of 6:1-29. This means that, in our text, there is no verse numbered Dan 6:29; rather, that content is found in 6:28.

Finally, in the VUL and TH versions, and partially in the OG, there are verses that follow chapter 12, which results in two additional chapters not typically included in the Protestant tradition. Thus, in the VUL and TH, for instance, there is a chapter 13, which contains the text often referred to as Susanna (here, too, the OG versification varies greatly from TH). Also, in chapter 14, the VUL and TH contain the history of Bel and the Dragon, which again, is not part of the Protestant tradition we are following. Thus, in our work, there is no text or translation provided for chapters 13 and 14. For translations of these, one might consult the NRSV or a version of the KJV that contains apocryphal literature. An end-result of the choices made here is that the text is, especially as concerns several points in chapter 4, a bit of a hodgepodge via extraction and conflation. If this were volume were text-critical in orientation, we might have made different choices. As it stands, however, the goal is to provide a helpful text for learners to be able to engage. We believe what we have provided here accomplishes that.

While the table above provides a convenient way to comprehend the versification in various versions of Daniel, it should still be noted that strict correspondence between the different texts often doesn't exist. Protestant tradition, nevertheless, at least from Dan 3:32-7:1, seems to follow the MT and TH. (nb: Because Susanna is not entirely relevant to this work, we have chosen not to provide an in-depth discussion of its versification. Additionally, it is worth mentioning here that I have used Bibleworks 10 to help work out matters of versification.)

Versification in Daniel					
OG	TH	NIV & KJV	VUL	MT (WTT)	GH
Old Greek	Theodotion	English	Latin Vulgate	Hebrew	GlossaHouse
		3:23			3:23 (OG)
3:24-90					
3:91			3:24		3:24 (91 OG)
3:92-97			3:25-30		3:25 (92 OG)-30 (97 OG)
	4:1-3		3:98-100	3:31-33	4:1-3 (TH)
4:4-5	4:4-5			4:1-2	4:4-5 (OG)
	4:6-7			4:3-4	4:6-7 (TH)
4:18	4:8			4:5	4:8-9 (18 OG)
	4:9			4:6	
4:10-32	4:10-32			4:7-29	4:10-32 (OG) *(Not Incl. 17a)*
4:33	4:33			4:30	4:33 (TH) *(Not Incl. 4:33a-b)*
4:34-35	4:34-35			4:31-32	4:34-35 (OG)
4:36	4:36			4:33	4:36 (OG)
4:37a-c	4:37			4:34	4:37 (TH)
5:1 Intro					
5:1-13 5:16-17 5:23 5:26-30			5:1-30		5:1-13 (OG) 5:16-17 (OG) 5:23 (OG) 5:26-30 (OG)
		6:1-29	5:31-6:28	6:1-29	5:31(6:1 OG)-6:28(29 OG)
		7:1-12:13			7:1-12:13 (OG)
*partial	13:1-65	See NRSV	13:1-65		
14:1-41	14:1-41	See NRSV	14:1-41		

Transliteration: Throughout this book we have transliterated names according to the "Koine Era Pronunciation" table provided on page ix (see also the discussion on "Pronunciation" below). Sometimes these will end up looking quite different than what is provided in most English versions. For instance, whereas most English Bibles contain names such as Joachim, Nebuchadnezzar, and Jerusalem, our version transliterates these names as Ioakim, Navoukhothonosor, and Ierousalem.

Punctuation: Other changes, particularly those dealing with capitalization and punctuation are provided in the following list identified first by chapter and then verse(s). Each of these changes was made to provide a more sensible and smooth reading of the text.

1:2 - Capitalized the second και as the start of a sentence; Removed comma after κυριου to treat the και...και construction like a both...and device
1:6 - Added the raised dot here before the list
1:10 - Added a raised dot to denote direct speech
1:11 - Added a raised dot to denote direct speech
1:12 - Replaced the raised dot with a period
1:16 - Replaced the raised dot with a period
1:18 - Replaced the raised dot with a period
1:19 - Replaced the raised dot with a period

2:2 - Replaced the comma after αὐτοῦ with a period.
2:3 - Added raised dot after βασιλεύς to denote direct speech
2:4 - Added raised dot after Συριστί to denote direct speech. Added comma between the two vocatives, Κύριε and Βασιλεῦ, to set each off. Also changed Βασιλεῦ from lower case to upper case. Replaced raised dot with period after ζῆθι.
2:6 - Replaced the raised dot with a period
2:8 - Replaced the raised dot with a period
2:9 - Replaced the raised dot with a period
2:10 - Replaced comma with a period after ἑώρακε
2:12 - Inserted comma after περίλυπος
2:13 - Replaced comma after ἀποκτεῖναι with period
2:15 - Inserted comma after λέγων
2:21 - Replaced the raised dot with a comma
2:22 - Replaced raised dot with period
2:26 - Made the δ in δυνήσῃ lower case
2:28 - Replaced period after ἐστι with a raised dot
2:44 - Replaced the comma with a period after the φθαρήσεται

3:8 - Added a period after Ἰουδαίους
3:9 - Added raised dot after εἶπον and replaced raised dot with a period after ζῆθι
3:11 - Replaced raised dot with a period after καιομένην
3:13 - Removed the period after βασιλέα
3:14 - Added a comma after οὕς; Added a raised dot after αὐτοῖς to denote direct speech
3:16 - Added a raised dot after Ναβουχοδονοσορ to denote direct speech
3:17 - Replaced the comma after σου with a raised dot (functioning as a semi-colon)
3:19 - Replaced raised dot after καῆναι with a period
3:23 - Replaced comma after ἀπέκτεινεν with a raised dot (functioning as a semi-colon)
3:24 - Added a raised dot after αὐτοῦ to denote direct speech

3:28 - Added a raised dot after εἶπεν to denote direct speech; Replaced raised dot after αὐτῶν with a period

4:1 - Added a raised dot after γῇ to denote direct speech; Added a period after πληθυνθείη
4:3 - Added a period after ἰσχυρά; Added a period after γενεάν
4:6 - Added a period after μοι
4:7 - Added a period after μοι
4:8-9 - Added a period after αὐτοῦ
4:14 - Added a raised dot after αὐτῷ to denote direct speech
4:15 - Added a raised dot after εἶπε to denote direct speech
4:30 - Added raised dot after εἶπεν to denote direct speech
4:31 - Added a raised dot after ἤκουσε to denote direct speech; Replaced raised dot after αὐτήν with a period and capitalized
4:32 - Replaced raised dot after ἀνθρώπου with a period and capitalized χόρτον
4:34 - Added a raised dot after λέγων to denote direct speech
4:35 - Added a period after ἐλογίσθησαν and capitalized καί; Added a period after γῆς and capitalized καί

5:7 - Added a raised dot after λέγων to denote direct speech
5:13 - Added a raised dot after αὐτῷ to denote direct speech
5:17 - Added a raised dot after βασιλεῖ to denote direct speech; Added a raised dot after γραφή to denote direct speech

6:1 - Replaced the raised dot after γήρει with a period
6:5 - Replaced the comma after βασιλέα with a period
6:6 - Removed the raised dot after ἀποθανεῖται
6:7 - Added a raised dot after βασιλέως to denote direct speech
6:13 - Added raised dot after εἶπαν to denote direct speech; Added a raised dot after αὐτοῖς to denote direct speech
6:13a - Added a raised dot after αὐτῷ to denote direct speech; Added a raised dot after εἶπεν to denote direct speech
6:14 - Added a raised dot after εἶπαν to denote direct speech
6:15 - Period after σατραπῶν to denote end of sentence
6:17 - Inserted raised dot after Δανιηλ to denote direct speech
6:21 - Added a raised dot after λέγων to denote direct speech
6:22 - Raised dot after εἶπεν to denote direct speech
6:26 - Added a raised dot after to λέγων denote direct speech
6:28 - Removed the unneeded comma after σῶσαι

7:1 - Added a raised dot after λόγων to denote reported speech
7:5 - Raised dot after εἶπεν to denote direct speech
7:16 - Added a raised dot after μοι to denote direct speech

7:23 - Removed the comma after τετάρτο and added a raised dot after ὅτι to denote speech

8:3 - Added a comma after Αιλαμ
8:13 - Added a raised dot after λαλοῦντι to denote direct speech
8:14 - Added a raised dot after αὐτῷ to denote direct speech
8:16 - Added a raised dot after εἶπεν to denote direct speech
8:17 - Added a raised dot after μοι to denote direct speech
8:19 - Added a raised dot after μοι to denote direct speech

9:22 - Added a raised dot after εἶπεν to denote direct speech

10:11 - Added a raised dot after εἶπέν to denote direct speech
10:12 - Added a raised dot after με to denote direct speech; Removed raised dot after from Δανιηλ as ὅτι is causal
10:14 - Added a raised dot after μοι to denote direct speech
10:16 - Added a raised dot after μου to denote direct speech
10:19 - Added a raised dot after μοι to denote direct speech; Added a raised dot after εἶπα to denote direct speech

10:20 - Added a raised dot after με to denote direct speech

11:1 - Raised dot after μοι to denote direct speech
11:10 - Removed unneeded period after υἱός

12:6 - Added a raised dot after Πότε to denote direct speech
12:7 - Added a raised dot after ποταμοῦ to denote direct speech; Changed the raised dot after συντελείας to a period
12:8 - Added a raised dot after εἶπα to denote direct speech
12:9 - Added a raised dot after μοι to denote direct speech

Translation: Throughout this book we have worked hard to gloss Greek terms with consistent English ones. We believe this will prove beneficial to all learners and readers. Thus, at the bottom of each page is the GlossaHouse English Version (GEV). This translation is fresh and fairly literal; we have attempted to preserve word order significance and accurately represent important features of the Greek text that are more emphasized and, therefore, more prominent. All of this was intended for the beginning student in mind, who may need help with Greek word meanings and understanding the significance of special constructions, like purpose, conditionals, and participles. In this translation work, we have applied current research on linguistics and Greek grammar, emphasis constructions, orality, performance, and social-cultural backgrounds.

We have sought to strike a balance between trying to translate the import (as far as we can gather) of every sentence element but yet not "over" translating and moving into commentary. Understand that every translation always entails interpretation. We checked each other on numerous decisions, sometimes convincing the other of our particular views, sometimes not, on how best to translate some word, phrase or construction. In the end, we are quite confident in the results, knowing that there will be things that have been missed and points for improvement and enhancement. Let us comment on various features and aspects of this translation.

Greek Word Order is preserved as long as this still makes "good" English sense, especially when some sort of prominence attended the fronted word order. For example, preserving the preverbal placement of adverbial modifiers often retains their prominence in Greek. Additionally, because of this, the beginning and intermediate student will often be able to readily recognize where the English glosses are for words and phrases.

Gender Inclusiveness is preserved as much as possible. In his book, *Art of the Start*, revered businessman and author Guy Kawasaki once said of gender-inclusive language, "If only defeating sexism were as simple as throwing in an occasional he/she, she, her, or hers."[1] While Kawasaki goes on to use the pronoun "he" as a literary "shortcut," again, here we have attempted to preserve inclusiveness as much as possible. To cite Kawasaki again, he says, "Don't look for sexism where none exists."[2] Thus, the Greek word ἄνθρωπος is most essentially a *human being* (BDAG 81.1), although often glossed and translated as "a man." Typically, ἄνθρωπος is translated as "a person" or in the plural "people."

Every Particle or **Conjunction** has been translated, including the very frequently occurring instances of καί and δέ. This has been a common fault of modern English Translations in general not to, sometimes with important interpretations at stake. Καί is marked +continuity but also +additive. When used adverbially as ascensive καί, this indicates additive emphasis and is often translated "also" or "even." Otherwise, καί is translated "and."

The conjunction δέ is marked +new development, but can be used with contrasts (very context specific), but otherwise was translated so as to indicate movement in narrative. Thus, the following words have been used: *well, thus, moreover, additionally, but, so* (used in consequential narrative development is implied contextually), and occasionally *and*. The conjunction ἵνα, when indicating purpose, we have attempted to typically render as *in order that*, which distinguishes it from result clauses (*so that*) or content clauses (*that*). There may be instances, however, where the sense of purpose, content, or result (much less common) were hard to distinguish (e.g., requests), so ἵνα may be translated simple as *that*. Finally, for purpose statements, since the notion of intention is pivotal, the English helping verb *would* is much preferable to *might* or *should*; this should be a corrective to learning that the subjunctive is a mood of possibility and can be translated with "might." We try, as best we can, to follow this rule of thumb.

Verb Tenses in the Indicative Mood are translated somewhat consistently, with the most variation occurring with the Imperfect (see below). In light of the ongoing debate on the significance of the Greek verb and Verbal Aspect, we have taken a fairly conservative approach. We understand that imperfective verbal aspect (incomplete, in progress, internal) occurs in the Present and Imperfect Tenses, perfective (or: aoristic) aspect (complete or completed, external) in the Aorist Tense, stative/resultative aspect (complex action with effects) in the Perfect and Pluperfect Tenses, and future aspect (expectation) in the Future Tense. Our goal was to allow transparency in the translation; it is not that we think the translations are the best way to translate this or that verb in this or that context in

---

[1] Guy Kawasaki, *The Art of the Start: The Time-Tested, Battle-Hardened Guide for Anyone Starting Anything* (NY: Penguin, 2004), 5.

[2] Ibid.

every instance, but rather we wanted transparency in the English tense translation to the underlying Greek tenses, in order to facilitate observation, and further research and conversation. That being said, however, it is our current understanding that the augment in the Indicative moods marks past time, or possibly only remoteness; however, such remoteness would in narrative most often indicate past time.

Non-Indicative Mood Verbs we have tried to render consistently, in order to, once again, promote observation and further research and conversation. For the Perfect Tense we attempted to convey a stative/resultative aspect (complex action with results); for the Present Tense, an imperfective aspect (in progress or incomplete); and for the Aorist Tense, a perfective (or: aoristic) aspect (complete or completed). These senses were sometimes quite difficult to convey and could easily encumber the translation. Participles are complex to translate, since they occur in a variety of constructions. Moreover, participles are not inherently marked for any semantic relationship, but the relationship must be discerned from broader context. Below are further discussions for translating participles, depending on their location and tense.

Pre-nuclear verb participles we translated as follows: when relative sequencing of events seemed the most basic relationship, then present tense participles are translated as contemporaneous ("while going along") and aorist tense participles as antecedent or time prior ("after going"). The same is generally true for Genitive Absolutes. If other such words were deemed necessary from contextual considerations to indicate special semantic relationship in English, these words (e.g., *thereby, by, although*) will be placed in italics to indicate their interpretive nature.

Post-nuclear verb participles, since they tend to further describe the activity of the nuclear verb, were simply translated as participles ("seeing, walking"). Where the semantic relation from the semantics of the verb and context was so clear that the render it so generically strained English sense, then we supplied a conjunction in italics to indicate the semantic sense.

Various Types of Marked Constructions that convey some sort of emphasis were translated in such a way as to indicate their importance. The examples in Daniel, of course, does not nearly exhaust the different ways that Greek can indicate emphasis and give more prominence to sentences elements or discourse features. More work is needed here; the following constructions were fairly clear to translate. Fronted attributive demonstratives (i.e., placed in front of their head substantive) are foregrounded. Consequently, we might have chosen (or not) to translate such instances using the adverb *very*. Redundant nominative personal pronouns emphasize the subject, since the verbal endings are already mark subject person. Such redundancy is indicated by adding –*self* to the subject. Emphatic negation with οὐ μή is often rendered *never ever* to capture the emphasis. Depending on the attending constructions, this is not always possible.

Rhetorical questions that indicate wither an expected affirmative or negative response are worded in such a way as to indicate as much, and then the response is placed within parentheses in italics with exclamation mark: (*No!*) or (*Surely, No!*) or (*Surely, yes!*). Remember the rule of MNOP: μή or μητί expects a negative answer (*Surely, No!*) and οὐ or οὐχί expects a positive answer (*Surely, yes!*). To see these rhetorical questions clearly in the English translation conveys the tone of disappointment, correction, surprise, or confrontation.

Recitative ὅτι is an optional phenomenon; direct speech may or may not be introduced by ὅτι. When ὅτι does occur, it likely sets off the statement for some discursive, pragmatic reason. Stephen H. Levinsohn proposes that it may help signal the culmination of an argument or, in John's Gospel, the explanation of previous teaching.[4] Most essentially, it would seem that recitative ὅτι is marked + prominence for introducing important direct speech, which may happen (often) to culminate a unit or explicate teaching. We have chosen to indicate the presence of recitative ὅτι by translating it with a near demonstrative pronoun "this: …", because "this: …" sets off and anticipates what follows formally in English.

Pronunciation might seem like somewhat of an odd feature to include here but it is worthy of mention because it comes to bear on transliteration. The traditional transliteration of the term Ναβουχοδονοσορ is *Nebuchadnezzar*. Three points of difference arise here with the GEV: The Greek letter β is rendered with an English "v" instead of "b," the Greek letter δ is rendered with a soft "th" (as in "this"), and the Greek letter χ is rendered with "kh" instead of "ch." The resultant transliteration is Navoukhothonosor. We follow the principles of the Koine Era Pronunciation (KEP), rather thant he so-called Erasmian pronunciation, which is popular in the Western academic world, but is ultimately anachronistic and flawed. Thus, in spite of the myth that the pronunciation of Koine Greek cannot be recovered, we believe it can. Ultimately, this has bearing on how we go about the task of transliteration. It is our view that it is much more helpful if students, especially beginning students, are able to include correct historical approximations of sound in a letter-for-letter format when transliterating. Much more could be said about this matter but such is beyond the scope of this work. We have, however, included a table on the following page to assist with matters of pronunciation and transliteration.

Koine Era Pronunciation (KEP)

Alphabet

Letter	Transliteration	Pronunciation (Approx. Eng. Value/Sound)	Examples of Greek Words Transliterated
Α, α	A, a	ah – tor<u>ah</u>	λαμβάνω l<u>a</u>mvanō
Β, β	V, v	v – <u>v</u>et	λαμβάνω lam<u>v</u>anō
Γ, γ	Y, y – before ε and ι Gh, gh – before other vowels	y – <u>y</u>et gh – <u>gh</u>ost (but softer)	ἅγιος a<u>y</u>iōs ἀγαθός a<u>gh</u>athōs
Δ, δ	Dh, dh or Th, th	dh – <u>th</u>e (no Eng. equiv.) th - <u>th</u>e	διά <u>dh</u>ia <u>th</u>ia
Ε, ε	E, e	eh – mikv<u>eh</u>	σέ, s<u>e</u>
Ζ, ζ	Z, z	z – <u>z</u>oo	ζῷον, <u>z</u>ōōn
Η, η	Ā, ā	āy – p<u>ay</u>	μή, m<u>ā</u>
Θ, θ	Th, th	th – <u>th</u>ink	θεός, <u>th</u>eōs
Ι, ι	I, i Y, y	ee – b<u>ee</u>t y – <u>y</u>es (often will begin words)	Ἰησοῦς <u>I</u>āsous
Κ, κ	K, k	k – <u>k</u>ey	καί, <u>k</u>ai
Λ, λ	L, l	l – <u>l</u>eg	λέγω, <u>l</u>egō
Μ, μ	M, m	m – <u>m</u>ad	μέν, <u>m</u>en
Ν, ν	N, n	n – <u>n</u>o	νῦν, <u>n</u>yn
Ξ, ξ	Ks, ks	ks – boo<u>ks</u>	ξένος, <u>ks</u>enōs
Ο, ο	Ō, ō	ō – g<u>o</u>	πρός, pr<u>ō</u>s
Π, π	P, p	p – <u>p</u>eek	παῖς, <u>p</u>ais
Ρ, ρ	R, r	r – <u>r</u>im (trill/roll)	ῥίζα, <u>r</u>iza
Σ, σ, ς	S, s	s – <u>s</u>it	σοῦ, <u>s</u>ou
Τ, τ	T, t	t – <u>t</u>ip	τίς, <u>t</u>is
Υ, υ	Y, y V, v – in diph-thongs following α, ε, η (i.e. αυ, ευ, ηυ)	eew – au j<u>us</u> (cf. οι) av – <u>a</u>vocado (αυ) ev – <u>e</u>very (ευ) āv – <u>ā</u>very (ηυ)	κύριος k<u>y</u>riōs (see vowel pairs for examples of these)
Φ, φ	F, f (or Ph, ph)	f – <u>f</u>it	φάγε, <u>f</u>age
Χ, χ	Kh, kh (or X, x)	kh – bac<u>kh</u>oe (slight guttural)	χάρις <u>kh</u>aris
Ψ, ψ	Ps, ps	ps – <u>ps</u>alm	ψώρα, <u>ps</u>ōra
Ω, ω	Ō, ō	ō – g<u>o</u>	ᾠόν, <u>ō</u>ōn

Vowel Pairs

Letters	Transliteration	Pronunciation (Approx. Eng. Value/Sound)
αι	ai	ai (= eh) – s<u>ai</u>d
αυ	av, af (before β, δ, γ, λ, μ, ν, ρ, ζ)	av – <u>a</u>vocado af - w<u>af</u>t
ει	ei	ee – b<u>ee</u>t
ευ	ev, ef (before β, δ, γ, λ, μ, ν, ρ, ζ)	ev – <u>e</u>very ef - l<u>ef</u>t
ηυ	āv, āf (before β, δ, γ, λ, μ, ν, ρ, ζ)	āv – <u>ā</u>very āf – s<u>āf</u>e
οι	oi	like "eew" in "jus" of French "au j<u>us</u>"
ου	ou	ou – c<u>ou</u>p
υι	ui	eew-ee – au j<u>us</u> + b<u>ee</u>t

Consonant Pairs

Letters	Transliteration	Pronunciation
γγ	ng	ng - ha<u>ng</u>
γκ	nk	nk - du<u>nk</u>
γχ	nkh	nkh - a<u>nkh</u>
γξ	nks	nks - tha<u>nks</u>
μβ	mv	mv - hu<u>mv</u>ee
ντ	nt	nt - a<u>nt</u> or: nd - a<u>nd</u>

Some Notes:
1) The pronunciation framework provided here is based on a number of data including, but certainly not limited to, discussions about pronunciation, spellings, and spelling interchanges in ancient writings.
2) There is no "rough breathing" (e.g the "h" sound in "ha" or "help" in Koine, which is often denoted by the rough breathing mark ʽΗ, ἡ.) Everything is smoothed over in the Koine era.

Δανιηλ Κεφ. Α΄

1 Ἐπὶ βασιλέως Ιωακιμ τῆς Ιουδαίας ἔτους τρίτου παραγενόμενος Ναβουχοδονοσορ βασιλεὺς Βαβυλῶνος εἰς Ιερουσαλημ ἐπολιόρκει αὐτήν. 2 καὶ παρέδωκεν αὐτὴν κύριος εἰς χεῖρας αὐτοῦ. Καὶ Ιωακιμ τὸν βασιλέα τῆς Ιουδαίας καὶ μέρος τι τῶν ἱερῶν σκευῶν τοῦ κυρίου

καὶ ἀπήνεγκεν αὐτὰ εἰς Βαβυλῶνα καὶ ἀπηρείσατο αὐτὰ ἐν τῷ εἰδωλίῳ αὐτοῦ.

1:1 During the reign of Ioakim of Ioudah, during the third year, Naboukhodonosor, King of Babylon, came into Jerusalem and he besieged it. 2 And the Lord gave it into his hands. And Ioakim, the King of Ioudah, both carried away part of the holy vessels of the Lord into Babylon and he set them up in his idol's temple.

3 καὶ εἶπεν ὁ βασιλεὺς Αβιεσδρι τῷ ἑαυτοῦ ἀρχιευνούχῳ ἀγαγεῖν αὐτῷ ἐκ τῶν υἱῶν τῶν μεγιστάνων τοῦ Ισραηλ καὶ ἐκ τοῦ βασιλικοῦ γένους καὶ ἐκ τῶν ἐπιλέκτων 4 νεανίσκους ἀμώμους καὶ εὐειδεῖς καὶ ἐπιστήμονας ἐν πάσῃ σοφίᾳ καὶ γραμματικοὺς καὶ συνετοὺς καὶ σοφοὺς καὶ ἰσχύοντας ὥστε εἶναι ἐν τῷ οἴκῳ τοῦ βασιλέως καὶ διδάξαι αὐτοὺς γράμματα καὶ διάλεκτον Χαλδαϊκὴ

5 καὶ δίδοσθαι αὐτοῖς ἔκθεσιν ἐκ τοῦ οἴκου τοῦ βασιλέως καθ' ἑκάστην ἡμέραν καὶ ἀπὸ τῆς βασιλικῆς τραπέζης καὶ ἀπὸ τοῦ οἴνου, οὗ πίνει ὁ βασιλεύς, καὶ ἐκπαιδεῦσαι αὐτοὺς ἔτη τρία καὶ ἐκ τούτων στῆσαι ἔμπροσθεν τοῦ βασιλέως.

6 καὶ ἦσαν ἐκ τοῦ γένους τῶν υἱῶν Ισραηλ τῶν ἀπὸ τῆς Ιουδαίας· Δανιηλ, Ανανιας, Μισαηλ, Αζαριας.

7 καὶ ἐπέθηκεν αὐτοῖς ὁ ἀρχιευνοῦχος ὀνόματα

τῷ μὲν Δανιηλ Βαλτασαρ

τῷ δὲ Ανανια Σεδραχ

καὶ τῷ Μισαηλ Μισαχ

καὶ τῷ Αζαρια Αβδεναγω.

8 καὶ ἐνεθυμήθη Δανιηλ ἐν τῇ καρδίᾳ ὅπως μὴ ἀλισγηθῇ ἐν τῷ δείπνῳ τοῦ βασιλέως καὶ ἐν ᾧ πίνει οἴνῳ,

καὶ ἠξίωσε τὸν ἀρχιευνοῦχον ἵνα μὴ συμμολυνθῇ.

3 And the King said to Abiesdri, his own chief eunuch, to bring to him from the sons of the leaders of Israel and from the royal lineage and from the choice soldiers 4 young men without blemish both handsome in outward appearance and skilled in all wisdom, both literate and intelligent, both wise and are just as strong in order to be in the house of the King, and to instruct them in the letters and language of Khaldaikian 5 and to give them leftovers from the house of the King according to each day and from the table of the King and from the wine, which the King drinks, and to train them for three years and, from those ones, to stand before the King. 6 And there were, from the tribes of the sons of Israel of Ioudah: Daniel, Ananias, Misael, Azarias. 7 And the chief eunuch set upon them names, to Daniel, Baltasar, moreover, to Ananias, Sedrakh, both to Misael, Misakh, and to Azarias, Avthenago. 8 And Daniel desired in his heart that he not be defiled by the meal of the king and by the wine, which he drank, and consulted the chief eunuch in order that he would not disgrace himself.

9 And the Lord gave Daniel honor and grace before the chief eunuch. 10 And the chief eunuch said to Daniel: "I fear my master, the king, the one distributing your food and your drink, lest he should, after seeing your faces, be perplexed at the sickness alongside your comrades, the other young men, and even I will be in danger by my own neck." 11 And Daniel said to Abiesdri, the one appointed chief eunuch over Daniel, Ananias, Misael, and Azarias: 12 "Now test your servants for ten days, and give us from the corn crops of the land to eat and drink. 13 And if our outward appearance should appear perplexing alongside the other young men, the ones eating of the meal of the King, so then, do as you desire to your servants." 14 And he did this with them in this manner and tested them for ten days. 15 Well, after ten days, the appearance of them appeared well and the exterior of the body better than the other young men, the ones eating the king's meal. 16 And Abiesdri began taking their meal and their wine and gave to them from the corn crops. 17 And the Lord gave these young men knowledge, both understanding and insight into all the every literary art. And to Daniel he gave understanding into every word, both in vision and dream, and into all wisdom. 18 Well, after these days, the King ordered to bring them, and they were lead by the chief eunuch before the King, Navoukhothonosor. 19 And the King spoke to them and he did not find among those wise men, ones similar to Daniel and Ananias and Misael and Azarias. And they continued on in the presence of the King.

20 καὶ ἐν παντὶ λόγῳ καὶ συνέσει καὶ παιδείᾳ, ὅσα ἐξήτησε παρ' αὐτῶν ὁ βασιλεύς, κατέλαβεν αὐτοὺς σοφωτέρους δεκαπλασίως ὑπὲρ τοὺς σοφιστὰς καὶ τοὺς φιλοσόφους τοὺς ἐν πάσῃ τῇ βασιλείᾳ αὐτοῦ. καὶ ἐδόξασεν αὐτοὺς ὁ βασιλεὺς καὶ κατέστησεν αὐτοὺς ἄρχοντας καὶ ἀνέδειξεν αὐτοὺς σοφοὺς παρὰ πάντας τοὺς αὐτοῦ ἐν πράγμασιν ἐν πάσῃ τῇ γῇ αὐτοῦ καὶ ἐν τῇ βασιλείᾳ αὐτοῦ.

21 καὶ ἦν Δανιηλ ἕως τοῦ πρώτου ἔτους τῆς βασιλείας Κύρου βασιλέως Περσῶν.

Κεφ. Β΄

1 Καὶ ἐν τῷ ἔτει τῷ δευτέρῳ τῆς βασιλείας Ναβουχοδονοσορ συνέβη εἰς ὁράματα καὶ ἐνύπνια ἐμπεσεῖν τὸν βασιλέα καὶ ταραχθῆναι ἐν τῷ ἐνυπνίῳ αὐτοῦ, καὶ ὁ ὕπνος αὐτοῦ ἐγένετο ἀπ' αὐτοῦ.

2 καὶ ἐπέταξεν ὁ βασιλεὺς εἰσενεχθῆναι τοὺς ἐπαοιδοὺς καὶ τοὺς μάγους καὶ τοὺς φαρμάκους τῶν Χαλδαίων ἀναγγεῖλαι τῷ βασιλεῖ τὰ ἐνύπνια αὐτοῦ. καὶ παραγενόμενοι ἔστησαν παρὰ τῷ βασιλεῖ.

3 καὶ εἶπεν αὐτοῖς ὁ βασιλεύς·

Ἐνύπνιον ἑώρακα καὶ ἐκινήθη μου τὸ πνεῦμα· ἐπιγνῶναι οὖν θέλω τὸ ἐνύπνιον.

4 καὶ ἐλάλησαν οἱ Χαλδαῖοι πρὸς τὸν βασιλέα Συριστί·

Κύριε, Βασιλεῦ, τὸν αἰῶνα ζῆθι. ἀνάγγειλον τὸ ἐνύπνιόν σου τοῖς παισί σου, καὶ ἡμεῖς σοι φράσομεν τὴν σύγκρισιν αὐτοῦ.

5 ἀποκριθεὶς δὲ ὁ βασιλεὺς εἶπε τοῖς Χαλδαίοις ὅτι

Ἐὰν μὴ ἀπαγγείλητέ μοι ἐπ' ἀληθείας τὸ ἐνύπνιον καὶ τὴν τούτου σύγκρισιν δηλώσητέ μοι, παραδειγματισθήσεσθε, καὶ ἀναληφθήσεται ὑμῶν τὰ ὑπάρχοντα εἰς τὸ βασιλικόν· 6 ἐὰν δὲ τὸ ἐνύπνιον διασαφήσητέ μοι καὶ τὴν τούτου σύγκρισιν ἀναγγείλητε, λήψεσθε δόματα παντοῖα καὶ δοξασθήσεσθε ὑπ' ἐμοῦ. δηλώσατέ μοι τὸ ἐνύπνιον καὶ κρίνατε.

7 ἀπεκρίθησαν δὲ ἐκ δευτέρου λέγοντες Βασιλεῦ, τὸ ὅραμα εἰπόν, καὶ οἱ παῖδές σου κρινοῦσι πρὸς ταῦτα.

8 καὶ εἶπεν αὐτοῖς ὁ βασιλεύς

20 And in every word and (matter of) understanding and service that the King sought from them, he deemed their skilled wisdom (to be) tenfold to the sophists and philosophers--those in all his kingdom. And the King honored them and put them in charge and appointed them wise before all those (serving) him in deed in all of his land and in his kingdom. 21 And Daniel was there until the first year of year of the reign of King Cyrus of the Persians. 2:1 And in the second year of the reign of Navoukhothonosor, a vision came and dream fell upon the King and he was troubled in his dream, and a (deep) sleep came upon him. 2 And the King ordered to be brought in the enchanters and the magi and sorcerers of the Khaldaions to report to the King his dreams. And after they entered they stood before the King. 3 And the King said to them: "I had a dream and it troubled my spirit; therefore, I want to know the dream." 4 And the Khaldaions spoke before the King in Syriac: "Lord, King, live into the age. Report your dream to your enchanters, and we ourselves will explain its interpretation." 5 Well, the King answered back to the Khaldaions saying this: "Unless you report with certainty the dream, and its interpretation you make clear to me, you will be made an example and the things in your treasury will be destroyed. 6 But if you clarify the dream for me and explain its interpretation, you will receive manifold gifts and you will be honored by me. Disclose to me the dream and interpret (it)." 7 Well, they answered back a second time saying, "King, say the dream, and your enchanters will interpret with reference to these things." 8 And the king said to them,

"With certainty, I know that you are buying time, even as you know that the thing is departing from me, so also, therefore, I have, in such a manner, let it be so. 9 Nevertheless, report the dream to me with certainty and disclose its interpretation, you will be struck by death. For you promised to make false words for me, until the time passed; now, therefore, if you say the word to me, that which I saw at night, I will know also that you will disclose its interpretation. 10 And the Khaldaions answered back to the King, this: "No one of this land is able to tell the King that which he saw. Just (what) you yourself saw, also every king and every ruler does not ask for a thing like this from every wise man and magi and Khaldaion. 11 And the word, which you are seeking, King, is weighty and dangerous, and there is no one who will disclose these things to the King, except an angel, who is not dwelling with all flesh; he is not able, from any other place, to do just as you expect. 12 After the King became gloomy and deeply sad, he ordered to bring out all the wise men of Babylon. 13 And he instructed all to be killed. Moreover, he searched for Daniel and all those with him with the intent to destroy them. 14 Then Daniel spoke with counsel and purpose, which he had, to Arioch, chief of the royal guard of the King, whom he ordered to bring the wise men of Babylon, 15 and he inquired of him saying, "For what reason is the King instructing harshly?" Then, the ordinance, Arioch made known to Daniel. 16 But Daniel went quickly and consulted with the King in order that he might be given time from the King..."

that he might also disclose everything to the King. 17 Then, after Daniel went into his house, to Ananias and Misael and Azaria, the companions, he explained everything. 18 And he called for a fast and (a time) of prayer to seek vengeance from the Most High Lord about this mystery, so that they might not be betrayed--Daniel and those with him--unto death with the wise men of Babylon. 19 Then, to Daniel in a dream on that same night, the mystery of the King was revealed clearly; then, Daniel blessed the Lord Most High 20 and cried out saying, "Blessed is the name of the great Lord unto the age, because of his wisdom and greatness; 21 even he himself changes seasons and times, while deposing kings and putting them in charge, giving wisdom to the wise and understanding to those who are in-the-know, 22 uncovering the deep and dark things and knowing the things in the darkness and the things in the light, and the resting place (is) in him. 23 To you, Lord of my fathers, I profess and exalt (you), because wisdom and prudence you have gaven to me, and now you have shown me what I consulted (about)--the things to disclose to the King." 24 Well, Daniel, after going to Ariokh, the one put in charge by the King to kill all the wise men of Babylon, said to him, "On the one hand, do not destroy the wise men of Babylon, but on the other hand take me to the King and I will disclose each thing to the King."

25 τότε Αριωχ κατὰ σπουδὴν εἰσήγαγεν τὸν Δανιηλ πρὸς τὸν βασιλέα καὶ εἶπεν αὐτῷ ὅτι

Εὕρηκα ἄνθρωπον σοφὸν ἐκ τῆς αἰχμαλωσίας τῶν υἱῶν τῆς Ιουδαίας, ὃς τῷ βασιλεῖ δηλώσει ἕκαστα.

26 ἀποκριθεὶς δὲ ὁ βασιλεὺς εἶπε τῷ Δανιηλ ἐπικαλουμένῳ δὲ Χαλδαϊστὶ Βαλτασαρ

δυνήσῃ δηλῶσαί μοι τὸ ὅραμα, ὃ εἶδον, καὶ τὴν τούτου σύγκρισιν;

27 ἐκφωνήσας δὲ ὁ Δανιηλ ἐπὶ τοῦ βασιλέως εἶπεν

Τὸ μυστήριον, ὃ ἑώρακεν ὁ βασιλεύς, οὐκ ἔστι σοφῶν καὶ φαρμάκων καὶ ἐπαοιδῶν καὶ γαζαρηνῶν ἡ δήλωσις, 28 ἀλλ' ἔστι θεὸς ἐν οὐρανῷ ἀνακαλύπτων μυστήρια, ὃς ἐδήλωσε τῷ βασιλεῖ Ναβουχοδονοσορ ἃ δεῖ γενέσθαι ἐπ' ἐσχάτων τῶν ἡμερῶν. βασιλεῦ, εἰς τὸν αἰῶνα ζῆθι· τὸ ἐνύπνιον καὶ τὸ ὅραμα τῆς κεφαλῆς σου ἐπὶ τῆς κοίτης σου τοῦτό ἐστι· 29 σύ, βασιλεῦ, κατακλιθεὶς ἐπὶ τῆς κοίτης σου ἑώρακας πάντα, ὅσα δεῖ γενέσθαι ἐπ' ἐσχάτων τῶν ἡμερῶν, καὶ ὁ ἀνακαλύπτων μυστήρια ἐδήλωσέ σοι ἃ δεῖ γενέσθαι. 30 κἀμοὶ δὲ οὐ παρὰ τὴν σοφίαν τὴν οὖσαν ἐν ἐμοὶ ὑπὲρ πάντας τοὺς ἀνθρώπους τὸ μυστήριον τοῦτο ἐξεφάνθη, ἀλλ' ἕνεκεν τοῦ δηλωθῆναι τῷ βασιλεῖ ἐσημάνθη μοι ἃ ὑπέλαβες τῇ καρδίᾳ σου ἐν γνώσει. 31 καὶ σύ, βασιλεῦ, ἑώρακας, καὶ ἰδοὺ εἰκὼν μία, καὶ ἦν ἡ εἰκὼν ἐκείνη μεγάλη σφόδρα, καὶ ἡ πρόσοψις αὐτῆς ὑπερφερὴς ἑστήκει ἐναντίον σου, καὶ ἡ πρόσοψις τῆς εἰκόνος φοβερά· 32 καὶ ἦν ἡ κεφαλὴ αὐτῆς ἀπὸ χρυσίου χρηστοῦ, τὸ στῆθος καὶ οἱ βραχίονες ἀργυροῖ, ἡ κοιλία καὶ οἱ μηροὶ χαλκοῖ, 33 τὰ δὲ σκέλη σιδηρᾶ, οἱ πόδες μέρος μέν τι σιδήρου, μέρος δέ τι ὀστράκινον. 34 ἑώρακας ἕως ὅτου ἐτμήθη λίθος ἐξ ὄρους ἄνευ χειρῶν καὶ ἐπάταξε τὴν εἰκόνα ἐπὶ τοὺς πόδας τοὺς σιδηροῦς καὶ ὀστρακίνους καὶ κατήλεσεν αὐτά. 35 τότε λεπτὰ ἐγένετο ἅμα ὁ σίδηρος καὶ τὸ ὄστρακον καὶ ὁ χαλκὸς καὶ ὁ ἄργυρος καὶ τὸ χρυσίον καὶ ἐγένετο ὡσεὶ λεπτότερον ἀχύρου ἐν ἅλωνι, καὶ ἐρρίπισεν αὐτὰ ὁ ἄνεμος ὥστε μηδὲν καταλειφθῆναι ἐξ αὐτῶν· καὶ ὁ λίθος ὁ πατάξας τὴν εἰκόνα ἐγένετο ὄρος μέγα καὶ ἐπάταξε πᾶσαν τὴν γῆν.

25 Then Ariokh, with haste, led Daniel to the King and said to him this: "I have found a wise man from among the captives of the sons of Ioudah, who will disclose each thing to the King." 26 Well, the King answered back, he said to Daniel, "Well, to the one being called in Khaldaian, Baltasar, are you able to disclose to me the dream, which I saw, and the interpretation of it?" 27 Well, Daniel cried out to the King, he said, "The mystery, which the King saw, there is not among the wise men and sorcerors and enchanters and diviners, the disclosure, 28 but God, who is in heaven, uncovered the mystery, which I will disclose to King Navoukhathonosor, that which must happen in the last days. King, live long into the age; the dream and the vision from your head upon your bed is this: 29 You, King, after lying on your bed, saw everything which must happen in the last days, and the uncoverer of mysteries will disclose to you that which must happen. 30 Moreover, even to me--not for being among the wise--to me, on behalf of all the men, this mystery was revealed, but (only) on account of the disclosure to the King was it shown to me, that which you received in your heart with knowledge. 31 And you, King, you saw and beheld one image, and it was a very great image, and its excellent appearance stood before you, and the appearance of the image (was) frightening. 32 And its head was of the finest gold, the chest and the arms silver, the stomach and thighs bronze, 33 moreover, the legs of iron, the feet, on the one hand part of iron, but on the other hand clay. 34 You watched until a rock was cut out from a mountain without hands and it struck the image upon the iron and clay feet and broke them into pieces. 35 Then, the remains happened to be along with the iron and clay, also the bronze and silver and gold, and like the small pieces of chaff on the threshing floor, the wind also ripped them up so as to leave none of them; and, the stone, the one that struck the image, became a great mountain and struck all the land.

36 τοῦτο τὸ ὅραμα· καὶ τὴν κρίσιν δὲ ἐροῦμεν ἐπὶ τοῦ βασιλέως. 37 σύ, βασιλεῦ βασιλεὺς βασιλέων, καὶ σοὶ ὁ κύριος τοῦ οὐρανοῦ τὴν ἀρχὴν καὶ τὴν βασιλείαν καὶ τὴν ἰσχὺν καὶ τὴν τιμὴν καὶ τὴν δόξαν ἔδωκεν, 38 ἐν πάσῃ τῇ οἰκουμένῃ ἀπὸ ἀνθρώπων καὶ θηρίων ἀγρίων καὶ πετεινῶν οὐρανοῦ καὶ τῶν ἰχθύων τῆς θαλάσσης παρέδωκεν ὑπὸ τὰς χεῖράς σου κυριεύειν πάντων, σὺ εἶ ἡ κεφαλὴ ἡ χρυσῆ. 39 καὶ μετὰ σὲ ἀναστήσεται βασιλεία ἐλάττων σου, καὶ τρίτη βασιλεία ἄλλη χαλκῆ, ἣ κυριεύσει πάσης τῆς γῆς. 40 καὶ βασιλεία τετάρτη ἰσχυρὰ ὥσπερ ὁ σίδηρος ὁ δαμάζων πάντα καὶ πᾶν δένδρον ἐκκόπτων, καὶ σεισθήσεται πᾶσα ἡ γῆ. 41 καὶ ὡς ἑώρακας τοὺς πόδας αὐτῆς μέρος μέν τι ὀστράκου κεραμικοῦ μέρος δέ τι σιδήρου, βασιλεία ἄλλη διμερὴς ἔσται ἐν αὐτῇ, καθάπερ εἶδες τὸν σίδηρον ἀναμεμειγμένον ἅμα τῷ πηλίνῳ ὀστράκῳ· 42 καὶ οἱ δάκτυλοι τῶν ποδῶν μέρος μέν τι σιδηροῦν μέρος δέ τι ὀστράκινον. μέρος τι τῆς βασιλείας ἔσται ἰσχυρὸν καὶ μέρος τι ἔσται συντετριμμένον. 43 καὶ ὡς εἶδες τὸν σίδηρον ἀναμεμειγμένον ἅμα τῷ πηλίνῳ ὀστράκῳ, συμμειγεῖς ἔσονται εἰς γένεσιν ἀνθρώπων, οὐκ ἔσονται δὲ ὁμονοοῦντες οὔτε εὐνοοῦντες ἀ ἥλοις, ὥσπερ οὐδὲ ὁ σίδηρος δύναται συγκραθῆναι τῷ ὀστράκῳ. 44 καὶ ἐν τοῖς χρόνοις τῶν βασιλέων τούτων στήσει ὁ θεὸς τοῦ οὐρανοῦ βασιλείαν ἄλλην, ἥτις ἔσται εἰς τοὺς αἰῶνας καὶ οὐ φθαρήσεται. καὶ αὕτη ἡ βασιλεία ἄλλο ἔθνος οὐ μὴ ἐάσῃ, πατάξει δὲ καὶ ἀφανίσει τὰς βασιλείας ταύτας, καὶ αὐτὴ στήσεται εἰς τὸν αἰῶνα, 45 καθάπερ ἑώρακας ἐξ ὄρους τμηθῆναι λίθον ἄνευ χειρῶν, καὶ συνηλόησε τὸ ὄστρακον, τὸν σίδηρον καὶ τὸν χαλκὸν καὶ τὸν ἄργυρον καὶ τὸν χρυσόν. ὁ θεὸς ὁ μέγας ἐσήμανε τῷ βασιλεῖ τὰ ἐσόμενα ἐπ' ἐσχάτων τῶν ἡμερῶν, καὶ ἀκριβὲς τὸ ὅραμα, καὶ πιστὴ ἡ τούτου κρίσις.

46 τότε Ναβουχοδονοσορ ὁ βασιλεὺς πεσὼν ἐπὶ πρόσωπον χαμαὶ προσεκύνησε τῷ Δανιηλ καὶ ἐπέταξε θυσίας καὶ σπονδὰς ποιῆσαι αὐτῷ.

36 This is the dream; and, the interpretation, moreover, we will interpret for the King. 37 You, King, King of kings, even to you the Lord of heaven has given you the rule and the kingdom and the power and the honor and the glory, 38 among all the inhabitants, from the men and beasts of the fields and birds of the sky and the fish of the sea, he gave unto your hands to rule all, you yourself are the golden head. 39 And after you will arise a kingdom inferior to you, even a third kingdom yet of bronze, that will rule over all the earth. 40 And a fourth kingdom, strong like iron, breaking everything and cutting down every tree, also will shake the entire earth. 41 And as you watched part of its feet, on the one hand some clay ceramic part, but on the other hand, some iron, another bipartite kingdom will be in it, just as you saw the iron mixed together with the clay vessel; 42 and the toes of the feet, some part (were), on the one hand, iron, but some, on the other hand, clay. Some part of the kingdom will be strong and some part will be broken. 43 And as you saw the iron mixed together with the clay vessel, their mixture will be into the generations of humanity, but they will neither harmonize nor ally with another, just as the iron is not able to mix with the clay. 44 and in the times of those kings, the God of heaven, will establish another kingdom, which will exist into the ages and will not be destroyed. And this same kingdom might never permit another nation, but it will beat and destroy these kingdoms and it will stand into the age, 45 just as you saw a stone cut from the mountain without hands, and it ground to powder the vessels, both the iron and the bronze, both the silver and the gold. The great God made signs to the King that will happen in the last days, and accurate is the dream, and reliable is this interpretation." 46 Then, King Navoukhothonosor, falling face first on the ground, worshipped Daniel and ordered a sacrifice and a drink offering to be made to him.

7 And at that time, when all the nations heard the sounds of the trumpets and all the echoes of music, while falling, all the nations, tribes and languages, worshipped the golden image, which Navoukhothonosor erected, across from this (place). 8 In that time, after Khaldaion men came, they brought charges against the Ioudaions. 9 And while taking (them) up, they said, "Lord, King, live into the age. 10 You, King, ordered and decided that all men, whoever might hear the sound of the trumpets and the echoes of music, after they fall, shall worship the golden image 11 and whoever, after they fall, would not worship, he will be thrown into the burning furnace fo fire. 12 Well, there are certain men, Ioudaions, whom you have put in charge of the regions of the Babylonians--Sedrakh, Misakh, Avthenago--those men do not fear your commandment and your idol they do not render due and to your golden image, which you erected, they do not worship." 13 Then Navoukhothonosor, after he became angry with anger, ordered to bring Sedrakh, Misakh, Avthenago; then, the men were brought before the King 14 whom, even after he recogized (them), King Navoukhothonosor said to them, "Why, Sedrakh, Misakh, Avthenago, to my gods, do you not render due and to the golden image, which I erected, do you not worship? 15 And now, on the one hand, if you are ready, together at the hearing of the trumpets and all the echoes of music, afterward fall to worship the golden image, which I erected;

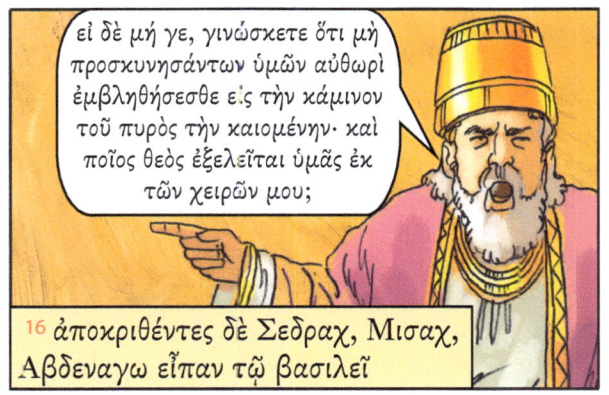

but, on the other hand, even if not, you know that if you yourselves do not worship, immediately you will be thrown into the burning furnace of fire; and what sort of God will deliver you from my hands?" 16 Well, after they answered back, Sedrakh, Misakh, Avthenago said to King Navoukhothonosor, "King, we ourselves do not have a need on the basis of this command, to answer you; 17 for, our God in the heavens is one Lord, whom we fear, who is able to deliver us from the furnace of fire, and out of your hands; King, he will deliver us. 18 And then it will be revealed to you, that neither your idol we render due nor your golden image, which you erected, we worship." 19 Then Navoukhothonosor was filled with anger, and his face changed for the worse, and he ordered to burn the furnace seven times more than it was usually necessary to burn. 20 And the strongest men of those able, he ordered, after they shackled the feet Sedrakh, Misakh, Avthenago, to throw (them) into the burning furnace of fire. 21 Then those men, after they were foot-shackled, while wearing their sandals and their turbans on their heads, along with their clothes, also were thrown into the furnace. 22 Since the ordinance of the King was urgent and the furnace was inflamed seven times more than previously, and the hand-picked men, after they foot-shackled them, led (them) to the furnace they and threw them into it. 23 On the one hand, therefore, after they foot-shackled those men they came around Azarias (and) the flame of the furnace burned and killed (them); on the other hand, they themselves were preserved. 24 And it happened in the hearing of the King, while they themselves were singing and standing, he saw (that) they themselves were living, then Navoukhothonosor, the King, marveled and stood up urgently and said to his friends:

25 "Behold, I myself saw four untied men walking in the fire, and not one happened to be destroyed among them, and the appearance of the fourth is like an angel of God." 26 And while the King was coming toward the door of the furnace burning with fire, he called them out by name--Sedrakh, Misakh, Avthenago, the servants of the God of gods, the Most High--he called them out of the fire. Thus, therefore, the men began coming out of the middle of the fire. 27 And they gathered together, the governors, the consuls, both the heads of families and the friends of the King, and they looked at those men, because neither the fire touched their bodies, and their hairs did not burn and their clothes were not changed, nor was the smell of fire on them. 28 Moreover, after he received (them), Navoukhothonosor, the King, said: "Blessed is the Lord, the God of Sedrakh, Misakh, Avthenago, who sent his messenger and saved his servants, the ones who hoped on him, for they rejected the command of the King and they gave up their bodies into the burning, in order that they would neither render due nor worship a god other than their God. 29 And now, I myself judge that every nation and every tribe and every language, whoever should blaspheme the Lord, the God of Sedrakh, Misakh, Avthenago, even his house will be dismembered (and) seized, because there is no other god who is able to deliver in this manner." 30 Therefore, in this manner, the King, gave to Sedrakh, Misakh, Avthenago, the whole region, he appointed them rulers.

1 Ναβουχοδονοσορ ὁ βασιλεὺς πᾶσι τοῖς λαοῖς φυλαῖς καὶ γλώσσαις τοῖς οἰκοῦσιν ἐν πάσῃ τῇ γῇ·

εἰρήνη ὑμῖν πληθυνθείη. 2 τὰ σημεῖα καὶ τὰ τέρατα ἃ ἐποίησεν μετ' ἐμοῦ ὁ θεὸς ὁ ὕψιστος ἤρεσεν ἐναντίον ἐμοῦ ἀναγγεῖλαι ὑμῖν. 3 ὡς μεγάλα καὶ ἰσχυρά. ἡ βασιλεία αὐτοῦ βασιλεία αἰώνιος καὶ ἡ ἐξουσία αὐτοῦ εἰς γενεὰν καὶ γενεάν.

4 Ἔτους ὀκτωκαιδεκάτου τῆς βασιλείας Ναβουχοδονοσορ εἶπεν

Εἰρηνεύων ἤμην ἐν τῷ οἴκῳ μου καὶ εὐθηνῶν ἐπὶ τοῦ θρόνου μου. 5 ἐνύπνιον εἶδον καὶ εὐλαβήθην, καὶ φόβος μοι ἐπέπεσεν. 6 καὶ δι' ἐμοῦ ἐτέθη δόγμα τοῦ εἰσαγαγεῖν ἐνώπιόν μου πάντας τοὺς σοφοὺς Βαβυλῶνος ὅπως τὴν σύγκρισιν τοῦ ἐνυπνίου γνωρίσωσίν μοι. 7 καὶ εἰσεπορεύοντο οἱ ἐπαοιδοὶ μάγοι γαζαρηνοὶ Χαλδαῖοι καὶ τὸ ἐνύπνιον εἶπα ἐγὼ ἐνώπιον αὐτῶν καὶ τὴν σύγκρισιν αὐτοῦ οὐκ ἐγνώρισάν μοι. 8-9 καὶ ἀναστὰς τὸ πρωὶ ἐκ τῆς κοίτης μου ἐκάλεσα τὸν Δανιηλ τὸν ἄρχοντα τῶν σοφιστῶν καὶ τὸν ἡγούμενον τῶν κρινόντων τὰ ἐνύπνια καὶ διηγησάμην αὐτῷ τὸ ἐνύπνιον καὶ ὑπέδειξέ μοι πᾶσαν τὴν σύγκρισιν αὐτοῦ. 10 ἐκάθευδον καὶ ἰδοὺ δένδρον ὑψηλὸν φυόμενον ἐπὶ τῆς γῆς· ἡ ὅρασις αὐτοῦ μεγάλη, καὶ οὐκ ἦν ἄλλο ὅμοιον αὐτῷ.

4:1 Navoukhothonosor, the King, to all peoples, tribes, and languages, to those living in all the land: "May peace be abundant among you. 2 The signs and the wonders, which the Most High God made for me, I am pleased to announce before you 3 as great and strong. His kingdom is an everlasting kingdom and his authority among generation and generation." 4 In the eighteenth year of King Navoukhothonosor, he said, "While being at peace, I was in my house and enjoying my throne. 5 I saw a dream and I became cautious, and fear fell upon me. 6 And the decree was given by me for all the wise men of Babylon to come before me in order that they would give the interpretation of the dream to me. 7 And they began entering--the enchanters, magi, Khaldaion treasurers--and I myself told the dream before them and the interpretation of it they did not tell me. 8-9 And after rising in the morning from my bed, I called Daniel, the chief of the wise men and rulers and interpreters, and I told the dreams to him, and he showed the dream to me and the interpretation of it. 10 I was lying down and, behold, a tall tree was growing above the ground; the appearance of it was great, and there was not another like it

11 And the appearance of it (was) great; the top of it nearly went up to the sky and the trunk of it nearly to the clouds, covering the things under the sky, the sun and moon were dwelling in it and it were giving light to all the land. 12 The branches of it (were) the length like thirty stadia, and under it all the beasts of the land were shading, and in it the birds of the sky nesting; the fruit of it much and good and provided for every animal. 13 I kept watching in my dream, and behold, an angel was sent in strength out of the sky 14 and he called and the same one said: 'Cut it down and destroy it; for, it has been commanded, from its highest point, to be uprooted and to make it worthless.' 15 And in this manner he said, 'Let one root of it (stay) in the ground, in order that the beasts of the land in these mountains, like cows, might consume the grass; 16 and, from the dew of the sky his body shall change, and (for) seven years he shall feed with them, 17 until when he shall know the Lord of the heaven has all authority in the heaven and upon the earth, and whatever he desires, he does in them.' 18 And after rising in the morning out of my bed, I called Daniel, the chief of the wise men and the ruler of the interpreters of dreams and told the story to him about the dream, and he showed me everything with reference to the interpretation of it. 19 Moreover, Daniel marveled greatly, and the suspicion kept agitating him, and after he had become afraid, after trembling took (hold) of him, and his appearance changed, he shook his head, after he marveled for one hour, he answered me back in a soft voice: 'King, this dream is for those hating you and the interpretation of it for those who have come as your enemies. 20 The tree, the one having been planted in the ground, which (was in) the great vision, is you yourself, King. 21 And all the birds of the sky, those ones nest in it; the strong of the land and of the nations and of all the languages up to the fathers of the lands and all the regions will be given to you.

34 καὶ ἐπὶ συντελείᾳ τῶν ἑπτὰ ἐτῶν ὁ χρόνος μου τῆς ἀπολυτρώσεως ἦλθε, καὶ αἱ ἁμαρτίαι μου καὶ αἱ ἄγνοιαί μου ἐπληρώθησαν ἐναντίον τοῦ θεοῦ τοῦ οὐρανοῦ· καὶ ἐδεήθην περὶ τῶν ἀγνοιῶν μου τοῦ θεοῦ τῶν θεῶν τοῦ μεγάλου, καὶ ἰδοὺ ἄγγελος εἷς ἐκάλεσέ με ἐκ τοῦ οὐρανοῦ λέγων· Ναβουχοδονοσορ, δούλευσον τῷ θεῷ τοῦ οὐρανοῦ τῷ ἁγίῳ καὶ δὸς δόξαν τῷ ὑψίστῳ· τὸ βασίλειον τοῦ ἔθνους σού σοι ἀποδίδοται. 35 καὶ πάντες οἱ κατοικοῦντες τὴν γῆν ὡς οὐδὲν ἐλογίσθησαν. Καὶ κατὰ τὸ θέλημα αὐτοῦ ποιεῖ ἐν τῇ δυνάμει τοῦ οὐρανοῦ καὶ ἐν τῇ κατοικίᾳ τῆς γῆς. Καὶ οὐκ ἔστιν ὃς ἀντιποιήσεται τῇ χειρὶ αὐτοῦ καὶ ἐρεῖ αὐτῷ τί ἐποίησας 36 ἐν ἐκείνῳ τῷ καιρῷ ἀποκατεστάθη ἡ βασιλεία μου ἐμοί, καὶ ἡ δόξα μου ἀπεδόθη μοι. 37 τῷ ὑψίστῳ ἀνθομολογοῦμαι καὶ αἰνῶ τῷ κτίσαντι τὸν οὐρανὸν καὶ τὴν γῆν καὶ τὰς θαλάσσας καὶ τοὺς ποταμοὺς καὶ πάντα τὰ ἐν αὐτοῖς· ἐξομολογοῦμαι καὶ αἰνῶ, ὅτι αὐτός ἐστι θεὸς τῶν θεῶν καὶ κύριος τῶν κυρίων καὶ βασιλεὺς τῶν βασιλέων, ὅτι αὐτὸς ποιεῖ σημεῖα καὶ τέρατα καὶ ἀλλοιοῖ καιροὺς καὶ χρόνους ἀφαιρῶν βασιλείαν βασιλέων καὶ καθιστῶν ἑτέρους ἀντ' αὐτῶν. 37 νῦν οὖν ἐγὼ Ναβουχοδονοσορ αἰνῶ καὶ ὑπερυψῶ καὶ δοξάζω τὸν βασιλέα τοῦ οὐρανοῦ ὅτι πάντα τὰ ἔργα αὐτοῦ ἀληθινὰ καὶ αἱ τρίβοι αὐτοῦ κρίσις καὶ πάντας τοὺς πορευομένους ἐν ὑπερηφανίᾳ δύναται ταπεινῶσαι.

1 Βαλτασαρ ὁ βασιλεὺς ἐποίησεν ἑστιατορίαν μεγάλην τοῖς ἑταίροις αὐτοῦ καὶ ἔπινεν οἶνον.

Κεφ. Ε

2 καὶ ἀνυψώθη ἡ καρδία αὐτοῦ, καὶ εἶπεν ἐνέγκαι τὰ σκεύη τὰ χρυσᾶ καὶ τὰ ἀργυρᾶ τοῦ οἴκου τοῦ θεοῦ, ἃ ἤνεγκε Ναβουχοδονοσορ ὁ πατὴρ αὐτοῦ ἀπὸ Ιερουσαλημ, καὶ οἰνοχοῆσαι ἐν αὐτοῖς τοῖς ἑταίροις αὐτοῦ.

34 And at the end of seven years, the time of my release came, and my sins and my ignorances were fulfilled in the presence of the God of heaven; and, I pleaded concerning my ignorances, from the great God of gods, and, behold, one angle called me from out of heaven saying: 'Novoukhothonosor, serve the holy God of heaven and give glory to the Most High; the kingdom of your nations is being given back to you.' 35 And everyone dwelling on the earth, they are reckoned as nothing. And according to his will he acts on the powerful of heaven and the dweller of the land. And there is not (one) who is able to stand against his hand and say to him, 'What have you done?' 36 In that moment, my kingdom was restored to me, and my glory returned to me. 37 To the Most High I give thanks and I praise the Creator of heaven and earth and the seas and the rivers and everything in them; I give thanks and I praise, because he himself is the God of gods and the Lord of lords and the King of kings, because he himself made signs and wonders and changes the seasons and times, removing kings of kingdoms and seating others in place of them. 37 Now, therefore, I myself, Navoukhothonosor, praise and exalt and glorify the King of heaven because all of his works are truth and his judgments just and everyone walking in arrogance he is able to humble. 5:1 King Baltasar made a great feast for his associates and drank wine. 2 And his heart rose, and he said to bring the gold and silver vessels of the house of God, which Navoukhothonosor, his father, brought from Jerusalem, and to pour wine in them for his associates.

καὶ ἔπινον ἐν αὐτοῖς

3 καὶ ἠνέχθη,

4 καὶ ηὐλόγουν τὰ εἴδωλα τὰ χειροποίητα αὐτῶν, καὶ τὸν θεὸν τοῦ αἰῶνος οὐκ εὐλόγησαν τὸν ἔχοντα τὴν ἐξουσίαν τοῦ πνεύματος αὐτῶν.

5 ἐν αὐτῇ τῇ ὥρᾳ ἐκείνῃ

ἐξῆλθον δάκτυλοι ὡσεὶ χειρὸς ἀνθρώπου καὶ ἔγραψαν ἐπὶ τοῦ τοίχου τοῦ οἴκου αὐτοῦ ἐπὶ τοῦ κονιάματος κατέναντι τοῦ φωτὸς ἔναντι τοῦ βασιλέως Βαλτασαρ, καὶ εἶδε χεῖρα γράφουσαν.

6 καὶ ἡ ὅρασις αὐτοῦ ἠλλοιώθη, καὶ φόβοι καὶ ὑπόνοιαι αὐτὸν κατέσπευδον. ἔσπευσεν οὖν ὁ βασιλεὺς καὶ ἐξανέστη καὶ ἑώρα τὴν γραφὴν ἐκείνην, καὶ οἱ συνέταιροι κύκλῳ αὐτοῦ ἐκαυχῶντο.

3 And they were brought, and they drank with them 4 and they blessed their handmade idols, and they did not bless the Everlasting God, the one having authority over their spirit. 5 In that same hour, out came fingers as if the hand of a person and wrote upon the wall of his house upon the plaster across from the light, toward King Baltasar, and he saw the hand writing. 6 And his apperance changed, and fear and suspicion dismayed him. Quickly, therefore, the King stood and kept looking at that writing, and the companions in a circle around him began talking loudly.

7 And the King spoke in a loud voice to call the enchanters and sorcerors and Khaldaions and diviners to announce the interpretation of the writing. And they entered to see the writing spectacle, and the interpretation of the writing they were not able to interpret for the King. Then, the King sent out a declaration saying: "Every man, who is able to show the meaning of the writing, he will robe him in purple and the gold necklace he will put around him, and to him will be give authority over a third of the kingdom." 8 And they entered, the enchanters and sorcerors and diviners, and no one was able to announce the interpretation of the writing. 9 Then the King called the queen about the sign and showed her, for it was great, and because all the people were not able to announce to the king the interpretation of the wirting. 10 Then the queen reminded him about Daniel, who was from the captives of Judea. 11 And she said to the King, "The person was knowledgeable and wise and surpassed all the wise men of Babylon, 12 and a holy spirit is in him, and in the days of your father, the King, he showed a difficult interpretation to Navoukhothonosor, your father.

13 τότε Δανιηλ εἰσήχθη πρὸς τὸν βασιλέα, καὶ ἀποκριθεὶς ὁ βασιλεὺς εἶπεν αὐτῷ·

16 Ὦ Δανιηλ, δύνῃ μοι ὑποδεῖξαι τὸ σύγκριμα τῆς γραφῆς;

καὶ στολιῶ σε πορφύραν

καὶ μανιάκην χρυσοῦν περιθήσω σοι,

καὶ ἕξεις ἐξουσίαν τοῦ τρίτου μέρους τῆς βασιλείας μου.

17 τότε Δανιηλ ἔστη κατέναντι τῆς γραφῆς καὶ ἀνέγνω καὶ οὕτως ἀπεκρίθη τῷ βασιλεῖ·

Αὕτη ἡ γραφή· Ἠρίθμηται, κατελογίσθη, ἐξῆρται· καὶ ἔστη ἡ γράψασα χείρ. καὶ αὕτη ἡ σύγκρισις αὐτῶν.

13 Then Daniel was brought in before the King, and answering the King said to him: 16 "O Daniel, are you able to show me the interpretation of the writing? I will both robe you in purple and put a gold necklance around you, and you will have authority over a third of the kingdom." 17 Then Daniel stood across from the writing and read and in this manner answered to the King: 'This (is) the writing: It has been numbered, it has been counted, it has been removed;' and the writing hand stood still. And this is their interpretation."

23 King, you yourself made a feast for your friends and drank wine, and the vessels of the house of the Living God were brought to you, and you drank with them, you and your nobles, and you praised all the handmade idols of humans; and you did not bless the Living God, and your spirit (is) in his hand, and your kingdom, he himself gave to you, and you neither blessed him nor praised him. 26-28 This is the interpretation of the writing: the time of your kingdom has been numbered, the fall of your kingdom, the end of your kingdom has been cut short, to the Medes and the Persians it will be given."

29 τότε Βαλτασαρ ὁ βασιλεὺς ἐνέδυσε τὸν Δανιηλ πορφύραν καὶ μανιάκην χρυσοῦν περιέθηκεν αὐτῷ καὶ ἔδωκεν ἐξουσίαν αὐτῷ τοῦ τρίτου μέρους τῆς βασιλείας αὐτοῦ. 30 καὶ τὸ σύγκριμα ἐπῆλθε Βαλτασαρ τῷ βασιλεῖ, καὶ τὸ βασίλειον ἐξῆρται ἀπὸ τῶν Χαλδαίων καὶ ἐδόθη τοῖς Μήδοις καὶ τοῖς Πέρσαις.

Κεφ. Ζ΄

1 καὶ Ἀρταξέρξης ὁ τῶν Μήδων παρέλαβε τὴν βασιλείαν. Καὶ Δαρεῖος πλήρης τῶν ἡμερῶν καὶ ἔνδοξος ἐν γήρει· 2 καὶ κατέστησε σατράπας ἑκατὸν εἴκοσι ἑπτὰ ἐπὶ πάσης τῆς βασιλείας αὐτοῦ

3 καὶ ἐπ᾽ αὐτῶν ἄνδρας τρεῖς ἡγουμένους αὐτῶν, καὶ Δανιηλ εἷς ἦν τῶν τριῶν ἀνδρῶν. 4 ὑπὲρ πάντας ἔχων ἐξουσίαν ἐν τῇ βασιλείᾳ. καὶ Δανιηλ ἦν ἐνδεδυμένος πορφύραν καὶ μέγας καὶ ἔνδοξος ἔναντι Δαρείου τοῦ βασιλέως, καθότι ἦν ἔνδοξος καὶ ἐπιστήμων καὶ συνετός, καὶ πνεῦμα ἅγιον ἐν αὐτῷ

καὶ εὐοδούμενος ἐν ταῖς πραγματείαις τοῦ βασιλέως, αἷς ἔπρασσε. τότε ὁ βασιλεὺς ἐβουλεύσατο καταστῆσαι τὸν Δανιηλ ἐπὶ πάσης τῆς βασιλείας αὐτοῦ καὶ τοὺς δύο ἄνδρας, οὓς κατέστησε μετ᾽ αὐτοῦ, καὶ σατράπας ἑκατὸν εἴκοσι ἑπτά.

5 ὅτε δὲ ἐβουλεύσατο ὁ βασιλεὺς καταστῆσαι τὸν Δανιηλ ἐπὶ πάσης τῆς βασιλείας αὐτοῦ, τότε βουλὴν καὶ γνώμην ἐβουλεύσαντο ἐν ἑαυτοῖς οἱ δύο νεανίσκοι πρὸς ἀλλήλους λέγοντες, ἐπεὶ οὐδεμίαν ἁμαρτίαν οὐδὲ ἄγνοιαν ηὕρισκον κατὰ τοῦ Δανιηλ περὶ ἧς κατηγορήσουσιν αὐτοῦ πρὸς τὸν βασιλέα.

29 Then Baltasar, the King, clothed Daniel in purple and put a gold necklace around him and he gave him authority over a third of his kingdom. 30 And the interpretation came upon Baltasar the King, and the kingdom was taken away from the Khaldaions and give to the Medes and the Persians. 6:1 And Artaxerxes, (King) of the Medes, took the kingdom. And Dareios grew full of days and esteemed in old age. 2 And he put in charge one hundred and twenty-seven satraps over all his kingdom 3 and over their men three of their leaders, and Daniel was one of the three men 4 having authority over all in the kingdom. And Daniel was clothed in purple and great and esteemed before Dareios, the King, because he was esteemed and loyal and clever, and a holy spirit (was) in him, and he prospered in the affairs of the King, which he carried out. Then the King decided put Daniel in charge of all his kingdom and the two men, whom he had been put in charge with, and the one hundred and twenty-seven satraps. 5 Well, whenever the King decided to put Daniel in charge over all his kingdom, then the two young men, among themselves, decided on a plan and verdict, saying to one another, because neither one sin nor ignorance did they find against Daniel about which they could accuse him to the King.

6 And they said, "Come, let's make a decree amongst ourselves that every person will neither make a worthy request and never pray a prayer to any God until after thirty days, except from Dareios, the King; otherwise, he shall die in order that Daniel would be defeated before the King, and would be thrown into the den of lions." For, they knew that Daniel prayed and pleaded with the Lord his God three times a day. 7 Then those men went and said in before the King: 8 "We have put in place a decree and statute that every man, whoever should pray a prayer or make some worthy request on behalf of any god until thirty days, except to Dareios, the King, would be thrown into the den of lions." 9 And they requested from the King in order that the statute and decree even he would not change it, since they knew that Daniel prayed and pleaded three times a day, in order that he might be proven inferior by the King and thrown into the den of lions. 10 And thus, King Dareios put (it) in place and confirmed (it). 11 Well, Daniel knew the decree, which was put in place against him, he opened the windows in his room, across from Jerusalem and fell on his face three times a day, just as he did before, and kept pleading.

12 And those same ones watched Daniel and caught him praying three times a day throughout each day. 13 Then these men met with the King and said: "King Dareios, did you not define a decree in order that any person would neither pray a prayer nor make a worthy request from any God besides you up to thirty days except for you, King; otherwise, moreover, he shall be thrown into the den of lions? Well, the King answered back, he said to them: 'The word is accurate, and the decree abides.'" 14 And they said: "Behold, we have found Daniel, your friend, praying and begging before his God three times a day." 15 And while grieving, the King said to thrown Daniel into the den of lions according to the decree, which was established according to him.

τότε ὁ βασιλεὺς σφόδρα ἐλυπήθη ἐπὶ τῷ Δανιηλ καὶ ἐβοήθει τοῦ ἐξελέσθαι αὐτὸν ἕως δυσμῶν ἡλίου ἀπὸ τῶν χειρῶν τῶν σατραπῶν.

13a καὶ εἶπον αὐτῷ·

Ὁρκίζομέν σε τοῖς Μήδων καὶ Περσῶν δόγμασιν, ἵνα μὴ ἀ οιώσῃς τὸ πρόσταγμα μηδὲ θαυμάσῃς πρόσωπον καὶ ἵνα μὴ ἐλαττώσῃς τι τῶν εἰρημένων καὶ κολάσῃς τὸν ἄνθρωπον, ὃς οὐκ ἐνέμεινε τῷ ὁρισμῷ τούτῳ.

καὶ εἶπεν·

Οὕτως ποιήσω καθὼς λέγετε, καὶ ἕστηκέ μοι τοῦτο.

16 καὶ οὐκ ἠδύνατο ἐξελέσθαι αὐτὸν ἀπ' αὐτῶν. 17 ἀναβοήσας δὲ Δαρεῖος ὁ βασιλεὺς εἶπε τῷ Δανιηλ·

Ὁ θεός σου, ᾧ σὺ λατρεύεις ἐνδελεχῶς τρὶς τῆς ἡμέρας, αὐτὸς ἐξελεῖταί σε ἐκ χειρὸς τῶν λεόντων· ἕως πρωὶ θάρρει.

18 τότε Δανιηλ ἐρρίφη εἰς τὸν λάκκον τῶν λεόντων, καὶ ἠνέχθη λίθος καὶ ἐτέθη εἰς τὸ στόμα τοῦ λάκκου,

καὶ ἐσφραγίσατο ὁ βασιλεὺς ἐν τῷ δακτυλίῳ ἑαυτοῦ

καὶ ἐν τοῖς δακτυλίοις τῶν μεγιστάνων αὐτοῦ, ὅπως μὴ ἀπ' αὐτῶν ἀρθῇ ὁ Δανιηλ ἢ ὁ βασιλεὺς αὐτὸν ἀνασπάσῃ ἐκ τοῦ λάκκου.

19 τότε ὑπέστρεψεν ὁ βασιλεὺς εἰς τὰ βασίλεια αὐτοῦ καὶ ηὐλίσθη νῆστις καὶ ἦν λυπούμενος περὶ τοῦ Δανιηλ. τότε ὁ θεὸς τοῦ Δανιηλ πρόνοιαν ποιούμενος αὐτοῦ ἀπέκλεισε τὰ στόματα τῶν λεόντων, καὶ οὐ παρηνώχλησαν τῷ Δανιηλ.

Then, the King was very grieved for Daniel and he desired to deliver him him up to the setting of the sun, from the hands of the satraps. 13a And they said to him: "We beg you, by ordinances of the Medes and the Persians, to neither change the matter nor respect the person and to not diminish some of the things you said, and you should punish the person, the one who did not abide by this decree." And he said: "Thus, I will do just as you say, and this has been established by me." 16 And he was not able to deliver him from them. 17 Well, after he cried out, Darieos, the King, said to Daniel: "Your God, to whom you yourself worshipped continually three times a day, that same one will deliver you from the hands of the lions; until morning, have courage!" 18 Then Daniel was thrown into the den of lions, and a stone was brought and set upon the mouth of the den, and the King sealed (it) with his ring and with the rings of his nobles, so that Daniel would not be taken away by them or the king lift him up out of the den. 19 Then the King returned to his kingdom and spent the night and he was said about Daniel. Then, the God of Daniel, acting providentially for him, closed the mouths of the lions and they did not trouble Daniel.

20 And the King, Dareios, rose early and went, with his satraps, and after going, stood at the mouth of the den of lions. 21 Then, the King called Daniel in a loud voice with wailing saying, "O Daniel, are you still alive, and your God, to whom you worshipped continually, did he save you from the lions, and did they not trouble you?" 22 Then, Daniel heard the loud voice and said, "King, I am still alive, 23 and God saved me from the lions, because allegiance was found in me before him; and, moreover, before you, King, neither ignorance nor sin was found in me; but, you yourself listened to people, deceivers of kings and threw me into the den of lions into destruction." 24 Then, all the powers-that-be gathered around and saw Daniel, as the lions had not troubled him.

25 τότε οἱ δύο ἄνθρωποι ἐκεῖνοι οἱ καταμαρτυρήσαντες τοῦ Δανιηλ, αὐτοὶ καὶ αἱ γυναῖκες αὐτῶν καὶ τὰ τέκνα αὐτῶν, ἐρρίφησαν τοῖς λέουσι, καὶ οἱ λέοντες ἀπέκτειναν αὐτοὺς καὶ ἔθλασαν τὰ ὀστᾶ αὐτῶν.

26 τότε Δαρεῖος ἔγραψε πᾶσι τοῖς ἔθνεσι καὶ χώραις καὶ γλώσσαις, τοῖς οἰκοῦσιν ἐν πάσῃ τῇ γῇ αὐτοῦ λέγων·

27 Πάντες οἱ ἄνθρωποι οἱ ὄντες ἐν τῇ βασιλείᾳ μου ἔστωσαν προσκυνοῦντες καὶ λατρεύοντες τῷ θεῷ τοῦ Δανιηλ, αὐτὸς γάρ ἐστι θεὸς μένων καὶ ζῶν εἰς γενεὰς γενεῶν ἕως τοῦ αἰῶνος· 28 ἐγὼ Δαρεῖος ἔσομαι αὐτῷ προσκυνῶν καὶ δουλεύων πάσας τὰς ἡμέρας μου, τὰ γὰρ εἴδωλα τὰ χειροποίητα οὐ δύνανται σῶσαι ὡς ἐλυτρώσατο ὁ θεὸς τοῦ Δανιηλ τὸν Δανιηλ.

29 καὶ ὁ βασιλεὺς Δαρεῖος προσετέθη πρὸς τὸ γένος αὐτοῦ, καὶ Δανιηλ κατεστάθη ἐπὶ τῆς βασιλείας Δαρείου· καὶ Κῦρος ὁ Πέρσης παρέλαβε τὴν βασιλείαν αὐτοῦ.

Κεφ. Ζ΄

1 Ἔτους πρώτου βασιλεύοντος Βαλτασαρ χώρας Βαβυλωνίας Δανιηλ ὅραμα εἶδε παρὰ κεφαλὴν ἐπὶ τῆς κοίτης αὐτοῦ·

τότε Δανιηλ τὸ ὅραμα, ὃ εἶδεν, ἔγραψεν εἰς κεφάλαια λόγων·

2 Ἐπὶ τῆς κοίτης μου ἐθεώρουν καθ᾽ ὕπνους νυκτὸς καὶ ἰδοὺ τέσσαρες ἄνεμοι τοῦ οὐρανοῦ ἐνέπεσον εἰς τὴν θάλασσαν τὴν μεγάλην. 3 καὶ τέσσαρα θηρία ἀνέβαινον ἐκ τῆς θαλάσσης διαφέροντα ἓν παρὰ τὸ ἕν. 4 τὸ πρῶτον ὡσεὶ λέαινα ἔχουσα πτερὰ ὡσεὶ ἀετοῦ· ἐθεώρουν ἕως ὅτου ἐτίλη τὰ πτερὰ αὐτῆς, καὶ ἤρθη ἀπὸ τῆς γῆς καὶ ἐπὶ ποδῶν ἀνθρωπίνων ἐστάθη, καὶ ἀνθρωπίνη καρδία ἐδόθη αὐτῇ.

25 Then, those two men, the false testifiers about Daniel, they and their wives and their children where thrown to the lions, and the lions destroyed them and broke their bones. 26 Then, Dareios wrote to all the nations and countries and languages, to the inhabitants in all his land saying: 27 "Every person, those existing in my kingdom, they shall fall prostrate and worship the God of Daniel, for he is an abiding and living God into the generations of generations up to the ages. 28 I myself, Dareios, will fall prostrate to and serve him all of my days, for the handmade idols are not able to save like the God who redeemed Daniel." 29 And King Dareios was added to his kind and Daniel was put in place over the kingdom of Dareios; and Cyrus, the Persian, received his kingdom. 7:1 In the first year while Baltasar was ruling the country of Babylonia, Daniel saw a vision from his head upon his bed; then, Daniel, the vision which he saw, he wrote a summary of the words. 2 "Upon my bed, I was watching in my sleep at night, and behold, four winds of the skies fell upon the Great Sea. 3 And four beasts rose out of the sea, each one differing from the (other) one. 4 The first was like a lioness, having wings like an eagle; I kept watching until feathers were plucked out of her, and it was lifted from the ground and put upon human feet, and a human heart was given to her.

5 καὶ ἰδοὺ μετ' αὐτὴν ἄλλο θηρίον ὁμοίωσιν ἔχον ἄρκου, καὶ ἐπὶ τοῦ ἑνὸς πλευροῦ ἐστάθη, καὶ τρία πλευρὰ ἦν ἐν τῷ στόματι αὐτῆς, καὶ οὕτως εἶπεν· Ἀνάστα κατάφαγε σάρκας πολλάς. 6 καὶ μετὰ ταῦτα ἐθεώρουν θηρίον ἄλλο ὡσεὶ πάρδαλιν, καὶ πτερὰ τέσσαρα ἐπέτεινεν ἐπάνω αὐτοῦ, καὶ τέσσαρες κεφαλαὶ τῷ θηρίῳ, καὶ γλῶσσα ἐδόθη αὐτῷ. 7 μετὰ δὲ ταῦτα ἐθεώρουν ἐν ὁράματι τῆς νυκτὸς θηρίον τέταρτον φοβερόν, καὶ ὁ φόβος αὐτοῦ ὑπερφέρων ἰσχύι, ἔχον ὀδόντας σιδηροῦς μεγάλους, ἐσθίον καὶ κοπανίζον, κύκλῳ τοῖς ποσὶ καταπατοῦν, διαφόρως χρώμενον παρὰ πάντα τὰ πρὸ αὐτοῦ θηρία· εἶχε δὲ κέρατα δέκα, 8 καὶ βουλαὶ πολλαὶ ἐν τοῖς κέρασιν αὐτοῦ. καὶ ἰδοὺ ἄλλο ἓν κέρας ἀνεφύη ἀνὰ μέσον αὐτῶν μικρὸν ἐν τοῖς κέρασιν αὐτοῦ, καὶ τρία τῶν κεράτων τῶν πρώτων ἐξηράνθησαν δι' αὐτοῦ· καὶ ἰδοὺ ὀφθαλμοὶ ὥσπερ ὀφθαλμοὶ ἀνθρώπινοι ἐν τῷ κέρατι τούτῳ καὶ στόμα λαλοῦν μεγάλα, καὶ ἐποίει πόλεμον πρὸς τοὺς ἁγίους. 9 ἐθεώρουν ἕως ὅτε θρόνοι ἐτέθησαν, καὶ παλαιὸς ἡμερῶν ἐκάθητο ἔχων περιβολὴν ὡσεὶ χιόνα, καὶ τὸ τρίχωμα τῆς κεφαλῆς αὐτοῦ ὡσεὶ ἔριον λευκὸν καθαρόν, ὁ θρόνος ὡσεὶ φλὸξ πυρός, 10 καὶ ἐξεπορεύετο κατὰ πρόσωπον αὐτοῦ ποταμὸς πυρός, χίλιαι χιλιάδες ἐθεράπευον αὐτὸν καὶ μύριαι μυριάδες παρειστήκεισαν αὐτῷ· καὶ κριτήριον ἐκάθισε καὶ βίβλοι ἠνεῴχθησαν. 11 ἐθεώρουν τότε τὴν φωνὴν τῶν λόγων τῶν μεγάλων, ὧν τὸ κέρας ἐλάλει, καὶ ἀπετυμπανίσθη τὸ θηρίον, καὶ ἀπώλετο τὸ σῶμα αὐτοῦ καὶ ἐδόθη εἰς καῦσιν πυρός. 12 καὶ τοὺς κύκλῳ αὐτοῦ ἀπέστησε τῆς ἐξουσίας αὐτῶν, καὶ χρόνος ζωῆς ἐδόθη αὐτοῖς ἕως χρόνου καὶ καιροῦ. 13 ἐθεώρουν ἐν ὁράματι τῆς νυκτὸς καὶ ἰδοὺ ἐπὶ τῶν νεφελῶν τοῦ οὐρανοῦ ὡς υἱὸς ἀνθρώπου ἤρχετο, καὶ ὡς παλαιὸς ἡμερῶν παρῆν, καὶ οἱ παρεστηκότες παρῆσαν αὐτῷ. 14 καὶ ἐδόθη αὐτῷ ἐξουσία, καὶ πάντα τὰ ἔθνη τῆς γῆς κατὰ γένη καὶ πᾶσα δόξα αὐτῷ λατρεύουσα· καὶ ἡ ἐξουσία αὐτοῦ ἐξουσία αἰώνιος, ἥτις οὐ μὴ ἀρθῇ, καὶ ἡ βασιλεία αὐτοῦ, ἥτις οὐ μὴ φθαρῇ. 15 καὶ ἀκηδιάσας ἐγὼ Δανιηλ ἐν τούτοις ἐν τῷ ὁράματι τῆς νυκτὸς 16 προσῆλθον πρὸς ἕνα τῶν ἑστώτων καὶ τὴν ἀκρίβειαν ἐζήτουν παρ' αὐτοῦ ὑπὲρ πάντων τούτων. ἀποκριθεὶς δὲ λέγει μοι καὶ τὴν κρίσιν τῶν λόγων ἐδήλωσέ μοι· 17 Ταῦτα τὰ θηρία τὰ μεγάλα εἰσὶ τέσσαρες βασιλεῖαι, αἳ ἀπολοῦνται ἀπὸ τῆς γῆς· 18 καὶ παραλήψονται τὴν βασιλείαν ἅγιοι ὑψίστου καὶ καθέξουσι τὴν βασιλείαν ἕως τοῦ αἰῶνος καὶ ἕως τοῦ αἰῶνος τῶν αἰώνων. 19 τότε ἤθελον ἐξακριβάσασθαι περὶ τοῦ θηρίου τοῦ τετάρτου τοῦ διαφθείροντος πάντα καὶ ὑπερφόβου, καὶ ἰδοὺ οἱ ὀδόντες αὐτοῦ σιδηροῖ καὶ οἱ ὄνυχες αὐτοῦ χαλκοῖ κατεσθίοντες πάντας κυκλόθεν καὶ καταπατοῦντες τοῖς ποσί, 20 καὶ περὶ τῶν δέκα κεράτων αὐτοῦ τῶν ἐπὶ τῆς κεφαλῆς καὶ τοῦ ἑνὸς τοῦ ἄλλου τοῦ προσφυέντος, καὶ ἐξέπεσαν δι' αὐτοῦ τρία, καὶ τὸ κέρας ἐκεῖνο εἶχεν ὀφθαλμοὺς καὶ στόμα λαλοῦν μεγάλα, καὶ ἡ πρόσοψις αὐτοῦ ὑπερέφερε τὰ ἄλλα.

5 And behold, after her, there was another beast similar to a bear, and it was placed one side, and there were three ribs in its mouth, and thus it was saying, "Rise, devour all flesh!" 6 And after these things, I was watching another beast like a leopard, also four bird wings were atop it, and four heads on the beast, and four languages were given to it. 7 Well, after these things, I kept watching in my vision at night a frightening fourth beast, and his fear was surpassing in strength, having great iron teeth, eating and snorting, stomping with its feet in a circle, acting differently than every beast before it; moreover, he had ten teeth, 8 And the group of horns (were) on his head. And, behold, another one, a horn, grew up in the middle of them, a small one on his head, and three of the first horns were withered by it; and, behold, human eyes (were) in this horn and a great speaking mouth, and it made war against the holy ones. 9 I kept watching until whenever the thrones were put in place, and an Ancient of Days sat, having a cloak like snow, and the hair of his head (was) like a sheep, pure white, the throne like a flame of fire, 10 and a river of fire flowed down from him, a thousand thousands were caring for him and ten thousand ten thousands were standing by him; and a judge was put in place and the books were opened. 11 I kept watching, then, a voice of great words, which the horn was saying, also destroyed the beast, and his body was destroyed and given to the burning fire. 12 And he removed those circled around him from their authority, and a time of life was given to them up to a time and a season. 13 I kept watching in the vision of the night and, behold, upon the clouds of the skies, (one) like a Son of Man was coming, and (one) like an Ancient of Days, and the ones standing beside were present with him. 14 And authority was given to him, and all the nations of the land by kind and all glory to him while worshipping; and, his authority is everlasting, which shall never be taken away, and his kingdom, which shall never perish. 15 And I, Daniel, after being exhausted by these things in the vision of the night, 16 I came near to one of those standing and sought precision from him about all of these things. Moreover, he spoke precisely to me and gave me the interpretation of the words: 17 'These great beasts are four kingdoms, which shall removed from the land; 18 and holy ones of the Most High will recieve the kingdom and possess the kingdom up to the age and into the age of ages. 19 Then, I wanted to be precise concerning the fourth beast, the one differing from all and frightening, and behold, his teeth (were) iron and his claws (were) bronze, devouring everything, circling and stomping with feet, 20 and concerning his ten horns on the head and the other one, the growing one, and on account of it three fell, and that horn had eyes and a great speaking mouth, and its appearance surpassed the others.

21 καὶ κατενόουν τὸ κέρας ἐκεῖνο πόλεμον συνιστάμενον πρὸς τοὺς ἁγίους καὶ τροπούμενον αὐτοὺς 22 ἕως τοῦ ἐλθεῖν τὸν παλαιὸν ἡμερῶν, καὶ τὴν κρίσιν ἔδωκε τοῖς ἁγίοις τοῦ ὑψίστου, καὶ ὁ καιρὸς ἐδόθη καὶ τὸ βασίλειον κατέσχον οἱ ἅγιοι. 23 καὶ ἐρρέθη μοι περὶ τοῦ θηρίου τοῦ τετάρτου ὅτι· βασιλεία τετάρτη ἔσται ἐπὶ τῆς γῆς, ἥτις διοίσει παρὰ πᾶσαν τὴν γῆν καὶ ἀναστατώσει αὐτὴν καὶ καταλεανεῖ αὐτήν. 24 καὶ τὰ δέκα κέρατα τῆς βασιλείας, δέκα βασιλεῖς στήσονται, καὶ ὁ ἄλλος βασιλεὺς μετὰ τούτους στήσεται, καὶ αὐτὸς διοίσει κακοῖς ὑπὲρ τοὺς πρώτους καὶ τρεῖς βασιλεῖς ταπεινώσει· 25 καὶ ῥήματα εἰς τὸν ὕψιστον λαλήσει καὶ τοὺς ἁγίους τοῦ ὑψίστου κατατρίψει καὶ προσδέξεται ἀλλοιῶσαι καιροὺς καὶ νόμον, καὶ παραδοθήσεται πάντα εἰς τὰς χεῖρας αὐτοῦ ἕως καιροῦ καὶ καιρῶν καὶ ἕως ἡμίσους καιροῦ. 26 καὶ ἡ κρίσις καθίσεται καὶ τὴν ἐξουσίαν ἀπολοῦσι καὶ βουλεύσονται μιᾶναι καὶ ἀπολέσαι ἕως τέλους. 27 καὶ τὴν βασιλείαν καὶ τὴν ἐξουσίαν καὶ τὴν μεγαλειότητα αὐτῶν καὶ τὴν ἀρχὴν πασῶν τῶν ὑπὸ τὸν οὐρανὸν βασιλειῶν ἔδωκε λαῷ ἁγίῳ ὑψίστου βασιλεῦσαι βασιλείαν αἰώνιον, καὶ πᾶσαι αἱ ἐξουσίαι αὐτῷ ὑποταγήσονται καὶ πειθαρχήσουσιν αὐτῷ. 28 ἕως καταστροφῆς τοῦ λόγου ἐγὼ Δανιηλ σφόδρα ἐκστάσει περιειχόμην, καὶ ἡ ἕξις μου διήνεγκεν ἐμοί, καὶ τὸ ῥῆμα ἐν καρδίᾳ μου ἐστήριξα.

Κεφ. η

1 Ἔτους τρίτου βασιλεύοντος Βαλτασαρ ὅρασις, ἣν εἶδον ἐγὼ Δανιηλ μετὰ τὸ ἰδεῖν με τὴν πρώτην. 2 καὶ εἶδον ἐν τῷ ὁράματι τοῦ ἐνυπνίου μου ἐμοῦ ὄντος ἐν Σούσοις τῇ πόλει, ἥτις ἐστὶν ἐν Ἐλυμαΐδι χώρᾳ, ἔτι ὄντος μου πρὸς τῇ πύλῃ Αιλαμ, 3 ἀναβλέψας εἶδον κριὸν ἕνα μέγαν ἑστῶτα ἀπέναντι τῆς πύλης, καὶ εἶχε κέρατα, καὶ τὸ ἓν ὑψηλότερον τοῦ ἑτέρου, καὶ τὸ ὑψηλότερον ἀνέβαινε. 4 μετὰ δὲ ταῦτα εἶδον τὸν κριὸν κερατίζοντα πρὸς ἀνατολὰς καὶ πρὸς βορρᾶν καὶ πρὸς δυσμὰς καὶ μεσημβρίαν, καὶ πάντα τὰ θηρία οὐκ ἔστησαν ἐνώπιον αὐτοῦ, καὶ οὐκ ἦν ὁ ῥυόμενος ἐκ τῶν χειρῶν αὐτοῦ, καὶ ἐποίει ὡς ἤθελε καὶ ὑψώθη. 5 καὶ ἐγὼ διενοούμην καὶ ἰδοὺ τράγος αἰγῶν ἤρχετο ἀπὸ δυσμῶν ἐπὶ προσώπου τῆς γῆς καὶ οὐχ ἥπτετο τῆς γῆς, καὶ ἦν τοῦ τράγου κέρας ἓν ἀνὰ μέσον τῶν ὀφθαλμῶν αὐτοῦ. 6 καὶ ἦλθεν ἐπὶ τὸν κριὸν τὸν τὰ κέρατα ἔχοντα, ὃν εἶδον ἑστῶτα πρὸς τῇ πύλῃ, καὶ ἔδραμε πρὸς αὐτὸν ἐν θυμῷ ὀργῆς. 7 καὶ εἶδον αὐτὸν προσάγοντα πρὸς τὸν κριόν, καὶ ἐθυμώθη ἐπ᾽ αὐτὸν καὶ ἐπάταξε καὶ συνέτριψε τὰ δύο κέρατα αὐτοῦ, καὶ οὐκέτι ἦν ἰσχὺς ἐν τῷ κριῷ στῆναι κατέναντι τοῦ τράγου· καὶ ἐσπάραξεν αὐτὸν ἐπὶ τὴν γῆν καὶ συνέτριψεν αὐτόν, καὶ οὐκ ἦν ὁ ῥυόμενος τὸν κριὸν ἀπὸ τοῦ τράγου. 8 καὶ ὁ τράγος τῶν αἰγῶν κατίσχυσε σφόδρα, καὶ ὅτε κατίσχυσε, συνετρίβη αὐτοῦ τὸ κέρας τὸ μέγα, καὶ ἀνέβη ἕτερα τέσσαρα κέρατα κατόπισθεν αὐτοῦ εἰς τοὺς τέσσαρας ἀνέμους τοῦ οὐρανοῦ. 9 καὶ ἐξ ἑνὸς αὐτῶν ἀνεφύη κέρας ἰσχυρὸν ἓν καὶ κατίσχυσε καὶ ἐπάταξεν ἐπὶ ἰσχυρὸν ἓν καὶ κατίσχυσε καὶ ἐπάταξεν ἐπὶ μεσημβρίαν καὶ ἐπ᾽ ἀνατολὰς καὶ ἐπὶ βορρᾶν· 10 καὶ ὑψώθη ἕως τῶν ἀστέρων τοῦ οὐρανοῦ, καὶ ἐρράχθη ἐπὶ ὑψώθη ἕως τῶν ἀστέρων τοῦ οὐρανοῦ, καὶ ἐρράχθη ἐπὶ τὴν γῆν ἀπὸ τῶν ἀστέρων καὶ ἀπὸ αὐτῶν κατεπατήθη, 11 ἕως ὁ ἀρχιστράτηγος ῥύσεται τὴν αἰχμαλωσίαν, καὶ δι᾽ αὐτὸν τὰ ὄρη τὰ ἀπ᾽ αἰῶνος ἐρράχθη, καὶ ἐξῄρθη ὁ τόπος αὐτῶν καὶ θυσία, καὶ ἔθηκεν αὐτὴν ἕως χαμαὶ ἐπὶ τὴν γῆν καὶ εὐωδώθη καὶ ἐγενήθη, καὶ τὸ ἅγιον ἐρημωθήσεται· 12 καὶ ἐγενήθησαν ἐπὶ τῇ θυσίᾳ αἱ ἁμαρτίαι, καὶ ἐρρίφη χαμαὶ ἡ δικαιοσύνη, καὶ ἐποίησε καὶ εὐωδώθη.

21 And I was watching that horn preparing for war for the holy ones and routing them 22 until the Ancient of Days came, and he gave the interpretation to the holy ones of the Most High, and he gave the season and the holy ones seized the kingdom. 23 And it was said to me concerning the fourth beast, this: 'There will be a fourth kingdom upon the land, which will prevail over all the land and unsettle and crush her. 24 And the ten horns of the kingdom, ten kings shall rise, and the other king shall rise after them, and the same one will prevail in evils over the first and he will humble three kings; 25 and he will speak words unto the Most High and he will exhuast the holy ones of the Most High and he will undertake to change seasons and laws, and everything will be given into his hands up to a season and seasons and half of a season. 26 And the judge will sit and destroy authority and decide to defile and destroy up to the end. 27 And the kingdom and the authority and the greatness of them and the rule of all of those under the sky of the kingdom, will be given to the holy people of the Most High to rule the kingdom (into) the age, and all the authorities to him will submit and obey him. 28 Until the catastrophe of the word, I, Daniel, overcome with great ecstacy, and my state spread within me, and the word was firm in my heart." 8:1 "In the third year, while Baltasar was ruling, there (was) a vision, which I myself, Daniel, saw after the first appeared to me. 2 And I saw in the vision of my dream, myself there in Sousa--the city, which is in the region of Elymais--myself there by the gate of Ailam, 3 after looking up, I saw a ram, a giant one, across from the gate, and it had horns, and the one was higher than the other, and the higher one stood out. 4 Well, after these things, I saw the ram charging to the east and to the north and to the west and to the south, and every beast did not stand before him, and not being rescued from his hands, and he was doing as he wanted and was exalted. 5 And I myself was thinking and, behold, a billygoat of the goats was coming from the west over the face of the land and he did not touch the land, and the horn of the billygoat, the one above it (had) eyes in the middle. 6 And it came upon the ram having the horns, which I saw standing by the gate, and it ran toward him in a furious rage. 7 And I saw him going toward the ram, and it was enraged by it and struck and crushed its two horns, and no longer was there strength in the horn to stand against the billygoat; and it attacked it upon the ground and crushed it, and not one was protecting the ram from the billygoat. 8 And the billygoat of the goats was exceedingly overpowering, and whenever he was overpowered, his great horn was crushed, and another four horns came up right behind it into the four winds of the sky. 9 And out of one of them sprouted one strong horn and it overpowered and struck upon the south and upon the east and upon the north. 10 And it was lifted up to the stars of the sky, and it was thrown down upon the ground from the stars and from them trampled, 11 until the chief star rescues the captives, and on acount of him the mountains, the everlasting ones, shall be shattered, and their place and sacrifice removed, and he put it in place on the ground upon the land and it grew, and the holy one shall be deserted. 12 And the sins were upon the sacrifice, and righteousness was thrown on the ground, and it acted and prospered.

13 καὶ ἤκουον ἑτέρου ἁγίου λαλοῦντος, καὶ εἶπεν ὁ ἕτερος τῷ φελμουνι τῷ λαλοῦντι· Ἕως τίνος τὸ ὅραμα στήσεται καὶ ἡ θυσία ἡ ἀρθεῖσα καὶ ἡ ἁμαρτία ἐρημώσεως ἡ δοθεῖσα, καὶ τὰ ἅγια ἐρημωθήσεται εἰς καταπάτημα; 14 καὶ εἶπεν αὐτῷ· Ἕως ἑσπέρας καὶ πρωὶ ἡμέραι δισχίλιαι τριακόσιαι, καὶ καθαρισθήσεται τὸ ἅγιον. 15 καὶ ἐγένετο ἐν τῷ θεωρεῖν με, ἐγὼ Δανιηλ, τὸ ὅραμα ἐζήτουν διανοηθῆναι, καὶ ἰδοὺ ἔστη κατεναντίον μου ὡς ὅρασις ἀνθρώπου. 16 καὶ ἤκουσα φωνὴν ἀνθρώπου ἀνὰ μέσον τοῦ Ουλαι, καὶ ἐκάλεσε καὶ εἶπεν· Γαβριηλ, συνέτισον ἐκεῖνον τὴν ὅρασιν. καὶ ἀναβοήσας εἶπεν ὁ ἄνθρωπος Ἐπὶ τὸ πρόσταγμα ἐκεῖνον ἡ ὅρασις. 17 καὶ ἦλθε καὶ ἔστη ἐχόμενός μου τῆς στάσεως, καὶ ἐν τῷ ἔρχεσθαι αὐτὸν ἐθορυβήθην καὶ ἔπεσα ἐπὶ πρόσωπόν μου, καὶ εἶπέν μοι· Διανοήθητι, υἱὲ ἀνθρώπου, ἔτι γὰρ εἰς ὥραν καιροῦ τοῦτο τὸ ὅραμα. 18 καὶ λαλοῦντος αὐτοῦ μετ' ἐμοῦ ἐκοιμήθην ἐπὶ πρόσωπον χαμαί, καὶ ἁψάμενός μου ἤγειρέ με ἐπὶ τοῦ τόπου 19 καὶ εἶπέ μοι· Ἰδοὺ ἐγὼ ἀπαγγέλλω σοι ἃ ἔσται ἐπ' ἐσχάτου τῆς ὀργῆς τοῖς υἱοῖς τοῦ λαοῦ σου· ἔτι γὰρ εἰς ὥρας καιροῦ συντελείας μενεῖ. 20 τὸν κριὸν ὃν εἶδες τὸν ἔχοντα τὰ κέρατα, βασιλεὺς Μήδων καὶ Περσῶν ἐστι. 21 καὶ ὁ τράγος τῶν αἰγῶν βασιλεὺς τῶν Ἑλλήνων ἐστί· καὶ τὸ κέρας τὸ μέγα τὸ ἀνὰ μέσον τῶν ὀφθαλμῶν αὐτοῦ, αὐτὸς ὁ βασιλεὺς ὁ πρῶτος. 22 καὶ τὰ συντριβέντα καὶ ἀναβάντα ὀπίσω αὐτοῦ τέσσαρα κέρατα, τέσσαρες βασιλεῖς τοῦ ἔθνους αὐτοῦ ἀναστήσονται οὐ κατὰ τὴν ἰσχὺν αὐτοῦ 23 καὶ ἐπ' ἐσχάτου τῆς βασιλείας αὐτῶν, πληρουμένων τῶν ἁμαρτιῶν αὐτῶν, ἀναστήσεται βασιλεὺς ἀναιδὴς προσώπῳ διανοούμενος αἰνίγματα. 24 καὶ στερεωθήσεται ἡ ἰσχὺς αὐτοῦ καὶ οὐκ ἐν τῇ ἰσχύι αὐτοῦ, καὶ θαυμαστῶς φθερεῖ καὶ εὐοδωθήσεται καὶ ποιήσει καὶ φθερεῖ δυνάστας καὶ δῆμον ἁγίων. 25 καὶ ἐπὶ τοὺς ἁγίους τὸ διανόημα αὐτοῦ, καὶ εὐοδωθήσεται τὸ ψεῦδος ἐν ταῖς χερσὶν αὐτοῦ, καὶ ἡ καρδία αὐτοῦ ὑψωθήσεται, καὶ δόλῳ ἀφανιεῖ πολλοὺς καὶ ἐπὶ ἀπωλείας ἀνδρῶν στήσεται καὶ ποιήσει συναγωγὴν χειρὸς καὶ ἀποδώσεται. 26 τὸ ὅραμα τὸ ἑσπέρας καὶ πρωὶ ηὑρέθη ἐπ' ἀληθείας· καὶ νῦν πεφραγμένον τὸ ὅραμα, ἔτι γὰρ εἰς ἡμέρας πολλάς. 27 ἐγὼ Δανιηλ ἀσθενήσας ἡμέρας πολλὰς καὶ ἀναστὰς ἐπραγματευόμην πάλιν βασιλικά. καὶ ἐξελυόμην ἐπὶ τῷ ὁράματι, καὶ οὐδεὶς ἦν ὁ διανοούμενος.

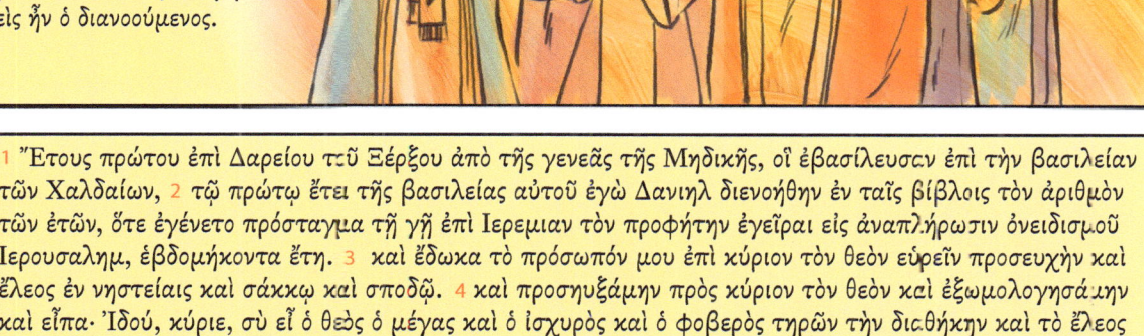

Κεφ. Θ'

1 Ἔτους πρώτου ἐπὶ Δαρείου τοῦ Ξέρξου ἀπὸ τῆς γενεᾶς τῆς Μηδικῆς, οἳ ἐβασίλευσαν ἐπὶ τὴν βασιλείαν τῶν Χαλδαίων, 2 τῷ πρώτῳ ἔτει τῆς βασιλείας αὐτοῦ ἐγὼ Δανιηλ διενοήθην ἐν ταῖς βίβλοις τὸν ἀριθμὸν τῶν ἐτῶν, ὅτε ἐγένετο πρόσταγμα τῇ γῇ ἐπὶ Ιερεμιαν τὸν προφήτην ἐγεῖραι εἰς ἀναπλήρωσιν ὀνειδισμοῦ Ιερουσαλημ, ἑβδομήκοντα ἔτη. 3 καὶ ἔδωκα τὸ πρόσωπόν μου ἐπὶ κύριον τὸν θεὸν εὑρεῖν προσευχὴν καὶ ἔλεος ἐν νηστείαις καὶ σάκκῳ καὶ σποδῷ. 4 καὶ προσηυξάμην πρὸς κύριον τὸν θεὸν καὶ ἐξωμολογησάμην καὶ εἶπα· Ἰδού, κύριε, σὺ εἶ ὁ θεὸς ὁ μέγας καὶ ὁ ἰσχυρὸς καὶ ὁ φοβερὸς τηρῶν τὴν διαθήκην καὶ τὸ ἔλεος τοῖς ἀγαπῶσί σε καὶ τοῖς φυλάσσουσι τὰ προστάγματά σου, 5 ἡμάρτομεν, ἠδικήσαμεν, ἠσεβήσαμεν καὶ ἀπέστημεν καὶ παρέβημεν τὰς ἐντολάς σου καὶ τὰ κρίματά σου 6 καὶ οὐκ ἠκούσαμεν τῶν παίδων σου τῶν προφητῶν, ἃ ἐλάλησαν ἐπὶ τῷ ὀνόματί σου ἐπὶ τοὺς βασιλεῖς ἡμῶν καὶ δυνάστας ἡμῶν καὶ πατέρας ἡμῶν καὶ παντὶ ἔθνει ἐπὶ τῆς γῆς. 7 σοί, κύριε, ἡ δικαιοσύνη, καὶ ἡμῖν ἡ αἰσχύνη τοῦ προσώπου κατὰ τὴν ἡμέραν ταύτην, ἀνθρώποις Ιουδα καὶ καθημένοις ἐν Ιερουσαλημ καὶ παντὶ τῷ λαῷ Ισραηλ τῷ ἔγγιστα καὶ τῷ ἀπωτέρω ἐν πάσαις ταῖς χώραις, εἰς ἃς διεσκόρπισας αὐτοὺς ἐκεῖ ἐν τῇ πλημμελείᾳ, ᾗ ἐπλημμέλησαν ἐναντίον σου. 8 δέσποτα, ἡμῖν ἡ αἰσχύνη τοῦ προσώπου καὶ τοῖς βασιλεῦσιν ἡμῶν καὶ δυνάσταις καὶ τοῖς πατράσιν ἡμῶν, ὅτι ἡμάρτομέν σοι.

13 And I kept hearing another holy one speaking, and the other said to Phelmouni, the one speaking: 'Until what (time) will the vision stand and the removed sacrifice and the given sin of desolation, and the holy ones be desloated by trampling?' 14 And he said to him: 'Until evenings and mornings, two thousand three hundred days, and the holy place will be cleansed.' 15 And it happened, in my seeing, while I, Daniel, was seeking to understand the vision, and behold, there stood across from me an appearance like a human. 16 And I heard the voice of a human in the midst of Oulai, and he called and he said: 'Gabriel, help understand the vision.' And getting up the person said: 'The vision is about the decree.' 17 And he came and stood being by (the place) of my standing, and at his coming, I was afraid and fell on my face, and he said to me: 'Understand, son of man, for yet (is) the hour of time (for) this vision.' 18 And in his speaking with me, I slept on the face of the ground, and after he touched me, he woke me in this place 19 and he said to me, "Behold, I myself announce to you what will be at the end of the wrath to the sons of your people; for, yet remains the hour of the time of completion. 20 The ram, which you saw having the horn, is King of the Medes and Persians. 21 And the billygoat of the goats is King of the Greeks; and the great horn above the middle of his eye, he is the first king. 22 And the crushed ones and the ones coming up behind the four horns, (are) the four kings of his nations rising not according to his strength. 23 And upon the last (days) of their reign, during the fullness of their sins, a king of shameless face will arise, understanding the enigmas. 24 And his strength will be strengthened but not by his strength, and he will vigorously destroy and he will succeed, he will both do (this) and destroy the powerful and holy citizens. 25 And against the holy ones (is) his thought, and the lie will succeed by his hands, and his heart will be exalted, and by deceit he will destroy many and by the destruction of men he will stand and he will make a gathering by hand and repay. 26 The vision, at evening and morning, was told in truth; and, now, the vision is walled in, for yet (it is) many days. 27 I, Daniel, was weak many days and, after having risen, again was doing royal business. And I was weary about the vision, and there was not one comprehender." 9 1 "During the first year of Dareios of Xerxes of the line of the Medes, the ones reigning over the kingdom of the Khaldaions, 2 in the first year of his reign, I, Daniel, thought about the books, the number of years, when the decree to the land came to Jeremiah the prophet to arise for the fulfillment of the reproach of Jerusalem--seventy years. 3 And I gave my face to the Lord God, to find prayer and mercy in fasting and ashes and sackcloth. 4 And I prayed to the Lord God and confessed and said, 'Behold, Lord, you are the great and strong God and the feared one, keeping the covenant and mercy with those you love and those guarding your decree, 5 we have sinned, we have been unjust, we have been ungodly and departed from overlooked your commands and your judgments. 6 And we have not listened to your servants the prophets, what they said in your name about our kings and rulers and our fathers and all the nations of the land. 7 To you, Lord, (is) righteousness, and the shame of our face during this day, to the people of Judah and those sitting in Jerusalem and all the people of Israel, the ones near and the ones far in every region, into which you dispersed them there in trespasses, for they trespassed before you. 8 Master, to us (is) the shame of our face and to our kings and rulers and to our fathers, because we sinned against you.

9 τῷ κυρίῳ ἡ δικαιοσύνη καὶ τὸ ἔλεος, ὅτι ἀπέστημεν ἀπὸ σοῦ 10 καὶ οὐκ ἠκούσαμεν τῆς φωνῆς κυρίου τοῦ θεοῦ ἡμῶν κατακολουθῆσαι τῷ νόμῳ σου, ᾧ ἔδωκας ἐνώπιον Μωσῆ καὶ ἡμῶν διὰ τῶν παίδων σου τῶν προφητῶν. 11 καὶ πᾶς Ισραηλ ἐγκατέλιπε τὸν νόμον σου καὶ ἀπέστησαν τοῦ μὴ ἀκοῦσαι τῆς φωνῆς σου, καὶ ἐπῆλθεν ἐφ' ἡμᾶς ἡ κατάρα καὶ ὁ ὅρκος ὁ γεγραμμένος ἐν τῷ νόμῳ Μωσῆ παιδὸς τοῦ θεοῦ, ὅτι ἡμάρτομεν αὐτῷ. 12 καὶ ἔστησεν ἡμῖν τὰ προστάγματα αὐτοῦ, ὅσα ἐλάλησεν ἐφ' ἡμᾶς καὶ ἐπὶ τοὺς κριτὰς ἡμῶν, ὅσα ἔκρινας ἡμῖν, ἐπαγαγεῖν ἐφ' ἡμᾶς κακὰ μεγάλα, οἷα οὐκ ἐγενήθη ὑπὸ τὸν οὐρανὸν καθότι ἐγενήθη ἐν Ιερουσαλημ. 13 κατὰ τὰ γεγραμμένα ἐν διαθήκῃ Μωσῆ πάντα τὰ κακὰ ἐπῆλθεν ἡμῖν, καὶ οὐκ ἐξεζητήσαμεν τὸ πρόσωπον κυρίου θεοῦ ἡμῶν ἀποστῆναι ἀπὸ τῶν ἁμαρτιῶν ἡμῶν καὶ διανοηθῆναι τὴν δικαιοσύνην σου, κύριε. 14 καὶ ἠγρύπνησε κύριος ὁ θεὸς ἐπὶ τὰ κακὰ καὶ ἐπήγαγεν ἐφ' ἡμᾶς, ὅτι δίκαιος κύριος ὁ θεὸς ἡμῶν ἐπὶ πάντα, ὅσα ἂν ποιήσῃ, καὶ οὐκ ἠκούσαμεν τῆς φωνῆς αὐτοῦ. 15 καὶ νῦν, δέσποτα κύριε ὁ θεὸς ἡμῶν ὁ ἐξαγαγὼν τὸν λαόν σου ἐξ Αἰγύπτου τῷ βραχίονί σου τῷ ὑψηλῷ καὶ ἐποίησας σεαυτῷ ὄνομα κατὰ τὴν ἡμέραν ταύτην, ἡμάρτομεν, ἠγνοήκαμεν. 16 δέσποτα, κατὰ τὴν δικαιοσύνην σου ἀποστραφήτω ὁ θυμός σου καὶ ἡ ὀργή σου ἀπὸ τῆς πόλεώς σου Ιερουσαλημ ὄρους τοῦ ἁγίου σου, ὅτι ἐν ταῖς ἁμαρτίαις ἡμῶν καὶ ἐν ταῖς ἀγνοίαις τῶν πατέρων ἡμῶν Ιερουσαλημ καὶ ὁ δῆμός σου, κύριε, εἰς ὀνειδισμὸν ἐν πᾶσι τοῖς περικύκλῳ ἡμῶν. 17 καὶ νῦν ἐπάκουσον, δέσποτα, τῆς προσευχῆς τοῦ παιδός σου καὶ ἐπὶ τὰς δεήσεις μου, καὶ ἐπιβλεψάτω τὸ πρόσωπόν σου ἐπὶ τὸ ὄρος τὸ ἅγιόν σου τὸ ἔρημον ἕνεκεν τῶν δούλων σου, δέσποτα. 18 πρόσχες, κύριε, τὸ οὖς σου καὶ ἐπάκουσόν μου· ἄνοιξον τοὺς ὀφθαλμούς σου καὶ ἰδὲ τὴν ἐρήμωσιν ἡμῶν καὶ τῆς πόλεώς σου, ἐφ' ἧς ἐπεκλήθη τὸ ὄνομά σου ἐπ' αὐτῆς· οὐ γὰρ ἐπὶ ταῖς δικαιοσύναις ἡμῶν ἡμεῖς δεόμεθα ἐν ταῖς προσευχαῖς ἡμῶν ἐνώπιόν σου, ἀλλὰ διὰ τὸ σὸν ἔλεος, 19 κύριε, σὺ ἱλάτευσον. κύριε, ἐπάκουσον καὶ ποίησον καὶ μὴ χρονίσῃς ἕνεκα σεαυτοῦ, δέσποτα, ὅτι τὸ ὄνομά σου ἐπεκλήθη ἐπὶ τὴν πόλιν σου Σιων καὶ ἐπὶ τὸν λαόν σου Ισραηλ. 20 καὶ ἕως ἐγὼ ἐλάλουν προσευχόμενος καὶ ἐξομολογούμενος τὰς ἁμαρτίας μου καὶ τὰς ἁμαρτίας τοῦ λαοῦ μου Ισραηλ καὶ δεόμενος ἐν ταῖς προσευχαῖς ἐναντίον κυρίου θεοῦ μου καὶ ὑπὲρ τοῦ ὄρους τοῦ ἁγίου τοῦ θεοῦ ἡμῶν, 21 καὶ ἔτι λαλοῦντός μου ἐν τῇ προσευχῇ μου καὶ ἰδοὺ ὁ ἀνήρ, ὃν εἶδον ἐν τῷ ὕπνῳ μου τὴν ἀρχήν, Γαβριηλ, τάχει φερόμενος προσήγγισέ μοι ἐν ὥρᾳ θυσίας ἑσπερινῆς. 22 καὶ προσῆλθε καὶ ἐλάλησε μετ' ἐμοῦ καὶ εἶπεν· Δανιηλ, ἄρτι ἐξῆλθον ὑποδεῖξαί σοι διάνοιαν. 23 ἐν ἀρχῇ τῆς δεήσεώς σου ἐξῆλθε πρόσταγμα παρὰ κυρίου, καὶ ἐγὼ ἦλθον ὑποδεῖξαί σοι, ὅτι ἐλεεινὸς εἶ· καὶ διανοήθητι τὸ πρόσταγμα. 24 ἑβδομήκοντα ἑβδομάδες ἐκρίθησαν ἐπὶ τὸν λαόν σου καὶ ἐπὶ τὴν πόλιν Σιων συντελεσθῆναι τὴν ἁμαρτίαν καὶ τὰς ἀδικίας σπανίσαι καὶ ἀπαλεῖψαι τὰς ἀδικίας καὶ διανοηθῆναι τὸ ὅραμα καὶ δοθῆναι δικαιοσύνην αἰώνιον καὶ συντελεσθῆναι τὸ ὅραμα καὶ εὐφρᾶναι ἅγιον ἁγίων. 25 καὶ γνώσῃ καὶ διανοηθήσῃ καὶ εὐφρανθήσῃ καὶ εὑρήσεις προστάγματα ἀποκριθῆναι καὶ οἰκοδομήσεις Ιερουσαλημ πόλιν κυρίῳ. 26 καὶ μετὰ ἑπτὰ καὶ ἑβδομήκοντα καὶ ἑξήκοντα δύο ἀποσταθήσεται χρῖσμα καὶ οὐκ ἔσται, καὶ βασιλεία ἐθνῶν φθερεῖ τὴν πόλιν καὶ τὸ ἅγιον μετὰ τοῦ χριστοῦ, καὶ ἥξει ἡ συντέλεια αὐτοῦ μετ' ὀργῆς καὶ ἕως καιροῦ συντελείας· ἀπὸ πολέμου πολεμηθήσεται. 27 καὶ δυναστεύσει ἡ διαθήκη εἰς πολλούς, καὶ πάλιν ἐπιστρέψει καὶ ἀνοικοδομηθήσεται εἰς πλάτος καὶ μῆκος· καὶ κατὰ συντέλειαν καιρῶν καὶ μετὰ ἑπτὰ καὶ ἑβδομήκοντα καιροὺς καὶ ἑξήκοντα δύο ἔτη ἕως καιροῦ συντελείας πολέμου καὶ ἀφαιρεθήσεται ἡ ἐρήμωσις ἐν τῷ κατισχῦσαι τὴν διαθήκην ἐπὶ πολλὰς ἑβδομάδας· καὶ ἐν τῷ τέλει τῆς ἑβδομάδος ἀρθήσεται ἡ θυσία καὶ ἡ σπονδή, καὶ ἐπὶ τὸ ἱερὸν βδέλυγμα τῶν ἐρημώσεων ἔσται ἕως συντελείας, καὶ συντέλεια δοθήσεται ἐπὶ τὴν ἐρήμωσιν.

9 To the Lord (is) righteousness and mercy, because we departed from you 10 and we did not listen to the voice of the Lord our God, to follow your law, which you gave to before Moses and your servants the prophets. 11 And all Israel has forsaken your law and turned to not listen to your voice, and the curse came upon us and the written oath in the Law of Moses, the servant of God, because we sinned against him. 12 And he has put in place his decrees, which he spoke against us and against our judges, who judged us, by bringing upon us great evils, which have not happened by the heavans as has happened in Jerusalem. 13 According to the things written in the covenant of Moses, all the evils came upon us, and we did not seek the face of the Lord our God to turn away from our sins and to understand your righteousness, Lord. 14 And the Lord God kept watch over the evils and brought them upon us, because the Lord our God is righteous over everything, in whatever he does, and we did not listen to his voice. 15 And now, Master, Lord our God, the one who led your people out of Egypt by your uplifted arm and made for yourself a name according to that day, we have sinned, we did not know. 16 Master, according to your righteousness, may your anger and your wrath turn away from your city, Jerusalem, your holy mountain, because in our sins and in the ignorance of our fathers, Jerusalm and your citizens, Lord, became a disgramce among all our neighbors. 17 And now, listen, Master, to the prayer of your servant and all my beggings, and may your face turn with favor upon your holy mountain, near the wilderness of your servant, Master. 18 Listen, Lord, with your ears; indeed, listen to me. Open your eyes and behold our devastation and your city, upon which your name has been called within it; for, not by our righteouss deed do we beg in our prayers before you, but on account of your mercy, 19 Lord, be gracious. Lord, listen and act and do not waste time on account of yourself, Master, because your name is called upon in your city, Sion, and upon (by) your people, Israel. 20 And as I myself was speaking, praying and confessing my sins and the sins of the my people, Israel, and begging in prayers before the Lord my God and on behalf of the holy mountain of our God, 21 and yet in my speaking, in my prayer, behold, (there was) also a man, whom i had seen in my first dream--Gabriel--while being carried he quickly approached me at the hour of evening sacrifice. 22 And he came and he spoke with me and said: 'Daniel, just now I came to show you understanding. 23 In the beginning of your begging, the decree came from the Lord, and I myself came to show you, because you are shown mercy; and understand the decree. 24 Seventy weeks has been judged for you by your people and by the city of Sion to fulfill the sins and exhaust the injustices and to understand the vision to be given and for everlasting righteousness and to fulfill the vision and to gladden the holy of holies. 25 And you will know and understand and rejoice and find the decees to answer back and you will build Jerusalem, a city to the Lord. 26 And after seven and seventy (time) and sixty-two (years), an anointed will depart and will no (longer) be, and a king of the nations will destroy the city and the holy (place) with the annointed one, and his end will come with wrath even up to the time of the end; he will be warred upon by war. 27 And the covenant will rule over many, and again it will return and be rebuilt as flat and long; and according to the end of the times and after the seven and seventy times and sixty-two years until the fulfilled time of war, even the devastation will be destroyed in the prevailing of the covenant after many weeks; and in the end of the half of seven weeks, the sacrifice and the libation will cease, and in the temple there will be an abomination of desolations until the fulfillment, and the fulfillment will be given in the devastation."

Κεφ. Γ΄

1 Ἐν τῷ ἐνιαυτῷ τῷ πρώτῳ Κύρου τοῦ βασιλέως Περσῶν πρόσταγμα ἐδείχθη τῷ Δανιηλ, ὃς ἐπεκλήθη τὸ ὄνομα Βαλτασαρ, καὶ ἀληθὲς τὸ ὅραμα καὶ τὸ πρόσταγμα, καὶ τὸ πλῆθος τὸ ἰσχυρὸν διανοηθήσεται τὸ πρόσταγμα, καὶ διενοήθην αὐτὸ ἐν ὁράματι. 2 ἐν ταῖς ἡμέραις ἐκείναις ἐγὼ Δανιηλ ἤμην πενθῶν τρεῖς ἑβδομάδας· 3 ἄρτον ἐπιθυμιῶν οὐκ ἔφαγον, καὶ κρέας καὶ οἶνος οὐκ εἰσῆλθεν εἰς τὸ στόμα μου, ἔλαιον οὐκ ἠλειψάμην ἕως τοῦ συντελέσαι με τὰς τρεῖς ἑβδομάδας τῶν ἡμερῶν. 4 καὶ ἐγένετο τῇ ἡμέρᾳ τῇ τετάρτῃ καὶ εἰκάδι τοῦ μηνὸς τοῦ πρώτου, καὶ ἐγὼ ἤμην ἐπὶ τοῦ χείλους τοῦ ποταμοῦ τοῦ μεγάλου, ὅς ἐστι Τίγρης, 5 καὶ ἦρα τοὺς ὀφθαλμούς μου καὶ εἶδον καὶ ἰδοὺ ἄνθρωπος εἷς ἐνδεδυμένος βύσσινα καὶ τὴν ὀσφὺν περιεζωσμένος βυσσίνῳ, καὶ ἐκ μέσου αὐτοῦ φῶς, 6 καὶ τὸ σῶμα αὐτοῦ ὡσεὶ θαρσις, καὶ τὸ πρόσωπον αὐτοῦ ὡσεὶ ὅρασις ἀστραπῆς, καὶ οἱ ὀφθαλμοὶ αὐτοῦ ὡσεὶ λαμπάδες πυρός, καὶ οἱ βραχίονες αὐτοῦ καὶ οἱ πόδες ὡσεὶ χαλκὸς ἐξαστράπτων, καὶ φωνὴ λαλιᾶς αὐτοῦ ὡσεὶ φωνὴ θορύβου. 7 καὶ εἶδον ἐγὼ Δανιηλ τὴν ὅρασιν τὴν μεγάλην ταύτην, καὶ οἱ ἄνθρωποι οἱ ὄντες μετ' ἐμοῦ οὐκ εἴδοσαν τὴν ὅρασιν ταύτην, καὶ φόβος ἰσχυρὸς ἐπέπεσεν ἐπ' αὐτούς, καὶ ἀπέδρασαν ἐν σπουδῇ· 8 καὶ ἐγὼ κατελείφθην μόνος καὶ εἶδον τὴν ὅρασιν τὴν μεγάλην ταύτην, καὶ οὐκ ἐγκατελείφθη ἐν ἐμοὶ ἰσχύς, καὶ ἰδοὺ πνεῦμα ἐπεστράφη ἐπ' ἐμὲ εἰς φθοράν, καὶ οὐ κατίσχυσα. 9 καὶ οὐκ ἤκουσα τὴν φωνὴν λαλιᾶς αὐτοῦ, ἐγὼ ἤμην πεπτωκὼς ἐπὶ πρόσωπόν μου ἐπὶ τὴν γῆν. 10 καὶ ἰδοὺ χεῖρα προσήγαγέ μοι καὶ ἤγειρέ με ἐπὶ τῶν γονάτων ἐπὶ τὰ ἴχνη τῶν ποδῶν μου. 11 καὶ εἶπέν μοι· Δανιηλ, ἄνθρωπος ἐλεεινὸς εἶ· διανοήθητι τοῖς προστάγμασιν, οἷς ἐγὼ λαλῶ ἐπὶ σε, καὶ στῆθι ἐπὶ τοῦ τόπου σου, ἄρτι γὰρ ἀπεστάλην ἐπὶ σέ. καὶ ἐν τῷ λαλῆσαι αὐτὸν μετ' ἐμοῦ τὸ πρόσταγμα τοῦτο ἔστην τρέμων. 12 καὶ εἶπεν πρός με· Μὴ φοβοῦ, Δανιηλ ὅτι ἀπὸ τῆς ἡμέρας τῆς πρώτης, ἧς ἔδωκας τὸ πρόσωπόν σου διανοηθῆναι καὶ ταπεινωθῆναι ἐναντίον κυρίου τοῦ θεοῦ σου, εἰσηκούσθη τὸ ῥῆμά σου, καὶ ἐγὼ εἰσῆλθον ἐν τῷ ῥήματί σου. 13 καὶ ὁ στρατηγὸς βασιλέως Περσῶν ἀνθειστήκει ἐναντίον μου εἴκοσι καὶ μίαν ἡμέραν, καὶ ἰδοὺ Μιχαηλ εἷς τῶν ἀρχόντων τῶν πρώτων ἐπῆλθε βοηθῆσαί μοι, καὶ αὐτὸν ἐκεῖ κατέλιπον μετὰ τοῦ στρατηγοῦ τοῦ βασιλέως Περσῶν. 14 καὶ εἶπέν μοι· Ἦλθον ὑποδεῖξαί σοι τί ὑπαντήσεται τῷ λαῷ σου ἐπ' ἐσχάτου τῶν ἡμερῶν, ἔτι γὰρ ὅρασις εἰς ἡμέρας. 15 καὶ ἐν τῷ αὐτὸν λαλῆσαι μετ' ἐμοῦ τὰ προστάγματα ταῦτα ἔδωκα τὸ πρόσωπόν μου ἐπὶ τὴν γῆν καὶ ἐσιώπησα. 16 καὶ ἰδοὺ ὡς ὁμοίωσις χειρὸς ἀνθρώπου ἥψατό μου τῶν χειλέων· καὶ ἤνοιξα τὸ στόμα μου καὶ ἐλάλησα καὶ εἶπα τῷ ἑστηκότι ἀπέναντί μου· Κύριε, καὶ ὡς ὅρασις ἐπεστράφη ἐπὶ τὸ πλευρόν μου ἐπ' ἐμέ, καὶ οὐκ ἦν ἐν ἐμοὶ ἰσχύς. 17 καὶ πῶς δυνήσεται ὁ παῖς λαλῆσαι μετὰ τοῦ κυρίου αὐτοῦ; καὶ ἐγὼ ἠσθένησα, καὶ οὐκ ἔστιν ἐν ἐμοὶ ἰσχύς, καὶ πνεῦμα οὐ κατελείφθη ἐν ἐμοί. 18 καὶ προσέθηκε καὶ ἥψατό μου ὡς ὅρασις ἀνθρώπου καὶ κατίσχυσέ με 19 καὶ εἶπέ μοι· Ἄνθρωπος ἐλεεινὸς εἶ, μὴ φοβοῦ, ὑγίαινε· ἀνδρίζου καὶ ἴσχυε. καὶ ἐν τῷ λαλῆσαι αὐτὸν μετ' ἐμοῦ ἴσχυσα καὶ εἶπα· Λαλησάτω ὁ κύριός μου, ὅτι ἐνίσχυσέ με. 20 καὶ εἶπεν πρός με· Γινώσκεις τί ἦλθον πρὸς σέ; καὶ νῦν ἐπιστρέψω διαμάχεσθαι μετὰ τοῦ στρατηγοῦ βασιλέως τῶν Περσῶν· καὶ ἐγὼ ἐξεπορευόμην, καὶ ἰδοὺ στρατηγὸς Ἑλλήνων εἰσεπορεύετο. 21 καὶ μάλα ὑποδείξω σοι τὰ πρῶτα ἐν ἀπογραφῇ ἀληθείας, καὶ οὐθεὶς ἦν ὁ βοηθῶν μετ' ἐμοῦ ὑπὲρ τούτων ἀλλ' ἢ Μιχαηλ ὁ ἄγγελος.

10:1 "In the first year of Kyrus, the King of the Persians, he gave a decree to Daniel, who was called by the name Baltasar, and true (was) the vision and the decree, and the strong multitude will understand the decree, and I understood in the vision. 2 In those days, I, Daniel, was myself in mourning three days. 3 I did not each choice food, and both meat and wine also did not enter into my mouth, I did not anoint (myself) with olive oil until my completion of the three weeks of days. 4 And it happened on the twenty-fourth day of the first month, and myself was on the bank of the great river, that is, the Tigris, 5 and I raised my eyes and saw and behold (there was) a man clothed in linen and the linen was surrounding (his) loin and waist, and from his midsection a shiny (buckle), 6 And his body (was) like thrasis, and his face like an apperance of lightning, and his eyes like lamps of fire, and his arms and feet like dazzling bronze, and the sound of his speaking like the sound of a crowd. 7 And I, Daniel, myself saw this great vision, and the people with me did not see this vision, and a strong fear fell upon them, and they ran away in haste; 8 and, I myself remained alone and saw this great vision, and strength did not remain in me, and behold, a spirit turned toward me as to corrupt, and I did not overcome (it). 9 And I did not hear the sound of his speaking, I myself fell put my face upon the ground. 10 And behold, he reached out a hand to me and raised me upon the knees upon the soles of my feet. 11 And he said to me: 'Daniel, you are a person shown mercy; think about the decrees which I myself told you about, and stand in your place, for just now I have sent to you.' And in his speaking with me about this command, I stood trembling. 12 And he said to me, 'Do not fear, Daniel, because from the first day, (on) which I put your face to know and to be humble before the Lord your God, your spoken word has been obeyed, and I myself came by the spoken word. 13 And the General of the King of the Persians stood against (and) before me, and behold, Michael, one of the first of the archangels, came to help me, and I left him there with the General of the King of the Persians. 14 And he said to me: 'I came to show you what will meet your people upon the last days, for yet (is) the vision for days.' 15 And in his speaking with me about these commands, I put my face upon the ground and was silent. 16 And behold, a hand as with the likeness of a person, touched my lips; and, I opened my mouth and spoke and talked to the one standing across from me: 'Lord, as the vision turned from my side upon me, there was not even strength in me; 17 and, how will the servant be able to speak with his lord?' And I myself became weak, and there was not strength in me, and the spirit did not remain in me. 18 And, in addition, he also touched me as the vision of a person overcame me 19 and he said to me: 'You are a man shown mercy, do not fear, be well; be manly and strong.' And in his speaking with me, I was strengthened and said, 'Let my Lord speak, because he has strengthened me.' 20 And he said before me: 'Do you know what came before you? And now, I will return to contend with the General of the King of the Persians; and I myself was leaving, and behold, the General of the Greeks was entering. 21 And I will especially show you the first things in the registry of truth, and there was no one with me helping but Michael, the angel.'"

Κεφ. ΙΑ΄

1 καὶ ἐν τῷ ἐνιαυτῷ τῷ πρώτῳ Κύρου τοῦ βασιλέως εἶπέν μοι· ἐνισχῦσαι καὶ ἀνδρίζεσθαι. 2 καὶ νῦν ἦλθον τὴν ἀλήθειαν ὑποδεῖξαί σοι. ἰδοὺ τρεῖς βασιλεῖς ἀνθεστήκασιν ἐν τῇ Περσίδι, καὶ ὁ τέταρτος πλουτήσει πλοῦτον μέγαν παρὰ πάντας· καὶ ἐν τῷ κατισχῦσαι αὐτὸν ἐν τῷ πλούτῳ αὐτοῦ ἐπαναστήσεται παντὶ βασιλεῖ Ἑλλήνων. 3 καὶ στήσεται βασιλεὺς δυνατὸς καὶ κυριεύσει κυριείας πολλῆς καὶ ποιήσει καθὼς ἂν βούληται. 4 καὶ ἐν τῷ ἀναστῆναι αὐτὸν συντριβήσεται ἡ βασιλεία αὐτοῦ καὶ μερισθήσεται εἰς τοὺς τέσσαρας ἀνέμους τοῦ οὐρανοῦ, οὐ κατὰ τὴν ἀλκὴν αὐτοῦ οὐδὲ κατὰ τὴν κυριείαν αὐτοῦ, ἣν ἐδυνάστευσε, ὅτι ἀποσταθήσεται ἡ βασιλεία αὐτοῦ, καὶ ἑτέρους διδάξει ταῦτα. 5 καὶ ἐνισχύσει βασιλείαν Αἰγύπτου· καὶ εἷς ἐκ τῶν δυναστῶν κατισχύσει αὐτὸν καὶ δυναστεύσει· δυναστεία μεγάλη ἡ δυναστεία αὐτοῦ. 6 καὶ εἰς συντέλειαν ἐνιαυτῶν ἄξει αὐτούς, καὶ εἰσελεύσεται βασιλεὺς Αἰγύπτου εἰς τὴν βασιλείαν τὴν βορρᾶ ποιήσασθαι συνθήκας· καὶ οὐ μὴ κατισχύσῃ, ὅτι ὁ βραχίων αὐτοῦ οὐ στήσει ἰσχύν, καὶ ὁ βραχίων αὐτοῦ ναρκήσει καὶ τῶν συμπορευομένων μετ' αὐτοῦ, καὶ μενεῖ εἰς ὥρας. 7 καὶ ἀναστήσεται φυτὸν ἐκ τῆς ῥίζης αὐτοῦ καθ' ἑαυτόν, καὶ ἥξει ἐπὶ τὴν δύναμιν αὐτοῦ ἐν ἰσχύι αὐτοῦ βασιλεὺς βορρᾶ καὶ ποιήσει ταραχὴν καὶ κατισχύσει. 8 καὶ τοὺς θεοὺς αὐτῶν καταστρέψει μετὰ τῶν χωνευτῶν αὐτῶν καὶ τοὺς ὄχλους αὐτῶν μετὰ τῶν σκευῶν τῶν ἐπιθυμημάτων αὐτῶν, τὸ ἀργύριον καὶ τὸ χρυσίον, ἐν αἰχμαλωσίᾳ ἀποίσουσιν εἰς Αἴγυπτον· καὶ ἔσται ἔτος βασιλεῖ βορρᾶ. 9 καὶ εἰσελεύσεται εἰς βασιλείαν Αἰγύπτου ἡμέρας· καὶ ἐπιστρέψει ἐπὶ τὴν γῆν αὐτοῦ 10 καὶ ὁ υἱὸς αὐτοῦ καὶ ἐρεθισθήσεται καὶ συνάξει συναγωγὴν ὄχλου πολλοῦ καὶ εἰσελεύσεται κατ' αὐτὴν κατασύρων· παρελεύσεται καὶ ἐπιστρέψει καὶ παροξυνθήσεται ἐπὶ πολύ. 11 καὶ ὀργισθήσεται βασιλεὺς Αἰγύπτου καὶ πολεμήσει μετὰ βασιλέως βορρᾶ, καὶ παραδοθήσεται ἡ συναγωγὴ εἰς τὰς χεῖρας αὐτοῦ· 12 καὶ λήψεται τὴν συναγωγήν, καὶ ὑψωθήσεται ἡ καρδία αὐτοῦ, καὶ ταράξει πολλοὺς καὶ οὐ μὴ φοβηθῇ. 13 καὶ ἐπιστρέψει βασιλεὺς βορρᾶ καὶ συνάξει πόλεως συναγωγὴν μείζονα παρὰ τὴν πρώτην κατὰ συντέλειαν καιροῦ ἐνιαυτοῦ καὶ εἰσελεύσεται εἰς αὐτὴν ἐπ' αὐτὸν ἐν ὄχλῳ πολλῷ καὶ ἐν χρήμασι πολλοῖς. 14 καὶ ἐν τοῖς καιροῖς ἐκείνοις διάνοιαι ἀναστήσονται ἐπὶ τὸν βασιλέα Αἰγύπτου· καὶ ἀνοικοδομήσει τὰ πεπτωκότα τοῦ ἔθνους σου καὶ ἀναστήσεται εἰς τὸ ἀναστῆσαι τὴν προφητείαν, καὶ προσκόψουσι. 15 καὶ ἐπελεύσεται βασιλεὺς βορρᾶ καὶ ἐπιστρέψει τὰ δόρατα αὐτοῦ καὶ λήψεται τὴν πόλιν τὴν ὀχυράν, καὶ οἱ βραχίονες βασιλέως Αἰγύπτου στήσονται μετὰ τῶν δυναστῶν αὐτοῦ, καὶ οὐκ ἔσται αὐτῷ ἰσχὺς εἰς τὸ ἀντιστῆναι αὐτῷ. 16 καὶ ποιήσει ὁ εἰσπορευόμενος ἐπ' αὐτὸν κατὰ τὸ θέλημα αὐτοῦ, καὶ οὐκ ἔσται ὁ ἀνθεστηκὼς ἐναντίον αὐτοῦ· καὶ στήσεται ἐν τῇ χώρᾳ, καὶ ἐπιτελεσθήσεται πάντα ἐν ταῖς χερσὶν αὐτοῦ. 17 καὶ δώσει τὸ πρόσωπον αὐτοῦ ἐπελθεῖν βίᾳ πᾶν τὸ ἔργον αὐτοῦ καὶ συνθήκας μετ' αὐτοῦ ποιήσεται· καὶ θυγατέρα ἀνθρώπου δώσει αὐτῷ εἰς τὸ φθεῖραι αὐτήν, καὶ οὐ πείσεται καὶ οὐκ ἔσται. 18 καὶ δώσει τὸ πρόσωπον αὐτοῦ ἐπὶ τὴν θάλασσαν καὶ λήψεται πολλοὺς καὶ ἐπιστρέψει ὀργὴν ὀνειδισμοῦ αὐτῶν ἐν ὅρκῳ κατὰ τὸν ὀνειδισμὸν αὐτοῦ. 19 ἐπιστρέψει τὸ πρόσωπον αὐτοῦ εἰς τὸ κατισχῦσαι τὴν χώραν αὐτοῦ καὶ προσκόψει καὶ πεσεῖται καὶ οὐχ εὑρεθήσεται. 20 καὶ ἀναστήσεται ἐκ τῆς ῥίζης αὐτοῦ φυτὸν βασιλείας εἰς ἀνάστασιν, ἀνὴρ τύπτων δόξαν βασιλέως· καὶ ἐν ἡμέραις ἐσχάταις συντριβήσεται καὶ οὐκ ἐν ὀργῇ οὐδὲ ἐν πολέμῳ.

1 And in the first year of the reign of Kyrus, he said to me: 'be strong and manly.' 2 And now I have to show the truth to you. Behold, three kings have risen up in Persia, and the fourth will be rich with great riches beyond all; and in his overcoming in his riches he will rise above all of the kings of the Greeks. 3 And a powerful king will stand and lord over many lords and he will do whatever he wants. 4 And in his rising up, his kingdom will be divided unto the four winds of the heavens, neither according to his courage nor according to his lordship, which he ruled, because his kingdom will be destroyed and he will teach others these things. 5 And the King of Egypt will grow strong; and one of the rulers will overpower him and he will rule; his rule (will be) a great rule. 6 And at the completion of the years, he will lead them, and the King of Egypt will enter into the Northern Kingdom to make an agreement; and he will never be overpowered, because his arm will not establish strength, and his arm will grow number and those associating with him, and he will remain for hours. 7 And a plant will rise up from out of its root against himself, and in his power in his strength, the King of the North will come and he will make turmoul and he will overcome. 8 And he will overturn their gods with their metal idols and their crowds with their desirous vessels, that of silver and gold, in shame they they will be carried into Egypt; and the King of the North will be for (so) for a year. 9 And he will enter into the kingdom of Egypt for days; and he will return to his land 10 and his son will also provoke his son and he will gather a gathering from a crowd of many and will enter in, rushing down against her; he will pass by and return and be provoked by much. 11 And the King of Egypt will be angry and wage war with the Northern King, and the gathering will be handed over into his hands. 12 And he will carry off the gathering, and his heart will be exalted, and he will trouble many and never be afraid. 13 And the Northern King will return and gather from the city a gathering, one greater than the first according to the fulfillment of the time of the year and he will into into it by it in a large crowed and with many things. 14 And in those times thoughts will arise about the King of Egypt; and he will rebuild the fallen of your nation and he will rise in order to raise up prophecy, and they will take offense. 15 And the Norther King will attack and turn his spears and take the fortified city, and the arms of the arms of the King of Egypt will stand with his powerful ones, and there will to be in him strength to stand against him. 16 And the one walking toward him will act according to his will, and there will not be one to oppose him; and he will stand in the the countryside, and everything will be completed by his hands. 17 And he will put his face to attack with force all his work and he will make an agreement with him; and he will give him a daughter of man to destroy her, and she will not stand and will not be. 18 And he will put his face to the sea and leave many and return wrath for their insult in an oath according to his insult. 19 He will put his face in order to strengthen his country and will strike and fall and be found no more. 20 And a royal plant will rise up out of his root in order to rise up, a man striking the glory of the King; and in the last days he will be broken and in wrath but not in war.

21 καὶ ἀναστήσεται ἐπὶ τὸν τόπον αὐτοῦ εὐκαταφρόνητος, καὶ οὐ δοθήσεται ἐπ' αὐτὸν δόξα βασιλέως· καὶ ἥξει ἐξάπινα, κατισχύσει βασιλεὺς ἐν κληροδοσίᾳ αὐτοῦ. 22 καὶ τοὺς βραχίονας τοὺς συντριβέντας συντρίψει ἀπὸ προσώπου αὐτοῦ. 23 καὶ μετὰ τῆς διαθήκης καὶ δήμου συνταγέντος μετ' αὐτοῦ ποιήσει ψεῦδος καὶ ἐπὶ ἔθνος ἰσχυρὸν ἐν ὀλιγοστῷ ἔθνει. 24 ἐξάπινα ἐρημώσει πόλιν καὶ ποιήσει ὅσα οὐκ ἐποίησαν οἱ πατέρες αὐτοῦ οὐδὲ οἱ πατέρες τῶν πατέρων αὐτοῦ· προνομὴν καὶ σκῦλα καὶ χρήματα αὐτοῖς δώσει καὶ ἐπὶ τὴν πόλιν τὴν ἰσχυρὰν διανοηθήσεται, καὶ οἱ λογισμοὶ αὐτοῦ εἰς μάτην. 25 καὶ ἐγερθήσεται ἡ ἰσχὺς αὐτοῦ καὶ ἡ καρδία αὐτοῦ ἐπὶ τὸν βασιλέα Αἰγύπτου ἐν ὄχλῳ πολλῷ, καὶ ὁ βασιλεὺς Αἰγύπτου ἐρεθισθήσεται εἰς πόλεμον ἐν ὄχλῳ ἰσχυρῷ σφόδρα λίαν· καὶ οὐ στήσεται, ὅτι διανοηθήσεται ἐπ' αὐτὸν διανοίᾳ. 26 καὶ καταναλώσουσιν αὐτὸν μέριμναι αὐτοῦ καὶ ἀποστρέψουσιν αὐτόν, καὶ παρελεύσεται καὶ κατασυριεῖ, καὶ πεσοῦνται τραυματίαι πολλοί. 27 καὶ δύο βασιλεῖς μόνοι δειπνήσουσιν ἐπὶ τὸ αὐτὸ καὶ ἐπὶ μιᾶς τραπέζης φάγονται καὶ ψευδολογήσουσι καὶ οὐκ εὐοδωθήσονται· ἔτι γὰρ συντέλεια εἰς καιρόν. 28 καὶ ἐπιστρέψει εἰς τὴν χώραν αὐτοῦ ἐν χρήμασι πολλοῖς, καὶ ἡ καρδία αὐτοῦ ἐπὶ τὴν διαθήκην τοῦ ἁγίου· ποιήσει καὶ ἐπιστρέψει ἐπὶ τὴν χώραν αὐτοῦ 29 εἰς καιρόν. καὶ εἰσελεύσεται εἰς Αἴγυπτον, καὶ οὐκ ἔσται ὡς ἡ πρώτη καὶ ἡ ἐσχάτη. 30 καὶ ἥξουσι Ῥωμαῖοι καὶ ἐξώσουσιν αὐτὸν καὶ ἐμβριμήσονται αὐτῷ· καὶ ἐπιστρέψει καὶ ὀργισθήσεται ἐπὶ τὴν διαθήκην τοῦ ἁγίου· καὶ ποιήσει καὶ ἐπιστρέψει καὶ διανοηθήσεται ἐπ' αὐτούς, ἀνθ' ὧν ἐγκατέλιπον τὴν διαθήκην τοῦ ἁγίου. 31 καὶ βραχίονες παρ' αὐτοῦ στήσονται καὶ μιανοῦσι τὸ ἅγιον τοῦ φόβου καὶ ἀποστήσουσι τὴν θυσίαν καὶ δώσουσι βδέλυγμα ἐρημώσεως. 32 καὶ ἐν ἁμαρτίαις διαθήκης μιανοῦσιν ἐν σκληρῷ λαῷ, καὶ ὁ δῆμος ὁ γινώσκων ταῦτα κατισχύσουσι καὶ ποιήσουσι. 33 καὶ ἐννοούμενοι τοῦ ἔθνους συνήσουσιν εἰς πολλούς· καὶ προσκόψουσι ῥομφαίᾳ καὶ παλαιωθήσονται ἐν αὐτῇ καὶ ἐν αἰχμαλωσίᾳ καὶ ἐν προνομῇ ἡμερῶν κηλιδωθήσονται. 34 καὶ ὅταν συντρίβωνται, συνάξουσιν ἰσχὺν βραχεῖαν, καὶ ἐπισυναχθήσονται ἐπ' αὐτοὺς πολλοὶ ἐπὶ πόλεως καὶ πολλοὶ ὡς ἐν κληροδοσίᾳ. 35 καὶ ἐκ τῶν συνιέντων διανοηθήσονται εἰς τὸ καθαρίσαι ἑαυτοὺς καὶ εἰς τὸ ἐκλεγῆναι καὶ εἰς τὸ καθαρισθῆναι ἕως καιροῦ συντελείας· ἔτι γὰρ καιρὸς εἰς ὥρας

21 And a despicable person will rise in his place, and he will royal glory will not be given to him; and he will come suddenly, the king will overcome in his his distributed land. 22 And he will break broken arms before his face; 23 and with the covenant and the populace, after an agreement with him, he will make a lie even before a strong nation by a smaller nation. 24 Suddenly, he will desolate the city and do that which none of his fathers did nor the fathers of his fathers; he will give plunder and spoil and things to them and he will think about the strong city, and his reasonings will be in vain. 25 Both his strength will rise and his heart by the King of Egypt with a large crowd, and the King of Egypt will be provoked into war with a very very strong crowd; and he will not stand, because a plot will be plotted against him. 26 And his worries will consume him and they will return to him, and he will depart and will be swept away, and many traumas will befall (him). 27 And the two kings will share a meal in the same place and they will eat at one table and they will speak lies and not prosper, for it is yet the fulfillment of time. 28 And he will return to his country with many things, and his heart will be against his holy covenant; he will act and return to his country 29 in time. And he will depart into Egypt, and the first will not be as the last. 30 And the Romans will come and they will expel him and be angry with him; and he will return and be angered against the holy covenant; and he will act and he will return and he will understand about them, for they abandoned the holy covenant. 31 And arms, from him, will rise and defile the holy (place) of fear and they will apostasize they sacrifice and give an abomination of desolation. 32 And in sin (against) the covenant, a people hard in heart will defile, and the knowing citizens will overcome this and act. 33 And the understanding ones of the nation will understand for many; and they will stumble by sword and will become old by it and in shame and in foraging they will be defiled for days. 34 And whenever they are broken, they will gather a little strength, and many of the city and many as in defilement will be gathered to them. 35 And out of the knowing, they will understand to cleanse themselves and to be chosen and to be cleansed until the fulfillment of time; for there is yet a time.

36 καὶ ποιήσει κατὰ τὸ θέλημα αὐτοῦ ὁ βασιλεὺς καὶ παροργισθήσεται καὶ ὑψωθήσεται ἐπὶ πάντα θεὸν καὶ ἐπὶ τὸν θεὸν τῶν θεῶν ἔξαλλα λαλήσει καὶ εὐοδωθήσεται, ἕως ἂν συντελεσθῇ ἡ ὀργή· εἰς αὐτὸν γὰρ συντέλεια γίνεται. 37 καὶ ἐπὶ τοὺς θεοὺς τῶν πατέρων αὐτοῦ οὐ μὴ προνοηθῇ καὶ ἐν ἐπιθυμίᾳ γυναικὸς οὐ μὴ προνοηθῇ, ὅτι ἐν παντὶ ὑψωθήσεται, καὶ ὑποταγήσεται αὐτῷ ἔθνη ἰσχυρά· 38 ἐπὶ τὸν τόπον αὐτοῦ κινήσει καὶ θεόν, ὃν οὐκ ἔγνωσαν οἱ πατέρες αὐτοῦ, τιμήσει ἐν χρυσίῳ καὶ ἀργυρίῳ καὶ λίθῳ πολυτελεῖ. καὶ ἐν ἐπιθυμήμασι 39 ποιήσει πόλεων καὶ εἰς ὀχύρωμα ἰσχυρὸν ἥξει· μετὰ θεοῦ ἀλλοτρίου, οὗ ἐὰν ἐπιγνῷ, πληθυνεῖ δόξαν καὶ κατακυριεύσει αὐτοῦ ἐπὶ πολὺ καὶ χώραν ἀπομεριεῖ εἰς δωρεάν. 40 καὶ καθ' ὥραν συντελείας συγκερατισθήσεται αὐτῷ ὁ βασιλεὺς Αἰγύπτου, καὶ ἐποργισθήσεται αὐτῷ βασιλεὺς βορρᾶ ἐν ἅρμασι καὶ ἐν ἵπποις πολλοῖς καὶ ἐν πλοίοις πολλοῖς καὶ εἰσελεύσεται εἰς χώραν Αἰγύπτου 41 καὶ ἐπελεύσεται εἰς τὴν χώραν μου, 42 καὶ ἐν χώρᾳ Αἰγύπτου οὐκ ἔσται ἐν αὐτῇ διασῳζόμενος. 43 καὶ κρατήσει τοῦ τόπου τοῦ χρυσίου καὶ τοῦ τόπου τοῦ ἀργυρίου καὶ πάσης τῆς ἐπιθυμίας Αἰγύπτου, καὶ Λίβυες καὶ Αἰθίοπες ἔσονται ἐν τῷ ὄχλῳ αὐτοῦ. 44 καὶ ἀκοὴ ταράξει αὐτὸν ἀπὸ ἀνατολῶν καὶ βορρᾶ, καὶ ἐξελεύσεται ἐν θυμῷ ἰσχυρῷ καὶ ῥομφαίᾳ ἀφανίσαι καὶ ἀποκτεῖναι πολλούς. 45 καὶ στήσει αὐτοῦ τὴν σκηνὴν τότε ἀνὰ μέσον τῶν θαλασσῶν καὶ τοῦ ὄρους τῆς θελήσεως τοῦ ἁγίου· καὶ ἥξει ὥρα τῆς συντελείας αὐτοῦ, καὶ οὐκ ἔσται ὁ βοηθῶν αὐτῷ.

36 And the King will act according to his will and be enraged and exalted over every god and god of gods, strange (things) he will say and he will propser, until when the wrath is fulfilled; for fulfillment unto him is coming. 37 And unto the gods of his fathers, he will never have regard and he will never desire for a wife, because in everything he will be exalted, and strong nations will submit to him. 38 By his place he will move even a god which his fathers did not know, he will honor it in gold and silver and valuable stone. And with desirable things 39 he will make from (various) cities and will come into a strong fortress; with a foreign god, whom he does not even know, he will add glory and rule over it by many (places), and he will divide many countries into parcels. 40 And according to the hour of fulfillment, the King of Egypt will lock horns with him, and be angry with him, the Northern King in chariots and on many horses and in many boats also will enter into the country of Egypt 41 and he will come upon my country, 42 and in the country of Egypt there will not be in it deliverance. 43 And he will seize the gold place and the silver place and all the desirous places of Egypt, and the Libyans and Ethiopians will be in his crowd. 44 And a report will warn him from the east and the north, and he will depart with a strong will and destroy by sword and to kill many. 45 And he will stand up his tent then between the middle of the seas and of the mountain of the holy one; and the hour of fulfillment will come, and there will be no helper for him."

Κεφ. ΙΒ΄

1 καὶ κατὰ τὴν ὥραν ἐκείνην παρελεύσεται Μιχαηλ ὁ ἄγγελος ὁ μέγας ὁ ἑστηκὼς ἐπὶ τοὺς υἱοὺς τοῦ λαοῦ σου· ἐκείνη ἡ ἡμέρα θλίψεως, οἵα οὐκ ἐγενήθη ἀφ᾽ οὗ ἐγενήθησαν ἕως τῆς ἡμέρας ἐκείνης· καὶ ἐν ἐκείνῃ τῇ ἡμέρᾳ ὑψωθήσεται πᾶς ὁ λαός, ὃς ἂν εὑρεθῇ ἐγγεγραμμένος ἐν τῷ βιβλίῳ. 2 καὶ πολλοὶ τῶν καθευδόντων ἐν τῷ πλάτει τῆς γῆς ἀναστήσονται, οἱ μὲν εἰς ζωὴν αἰώνιον, οἱ δὲ εἰς ὀνειδισμόν, οἱ δὲ εἰς διασπορὰν καὶ αἰσχύνην αἰώνιον. 3 καὶ οἱ συνιέντες φανοῦσιν ὡς φωστῆρες τοῦ οὐρανοῦ καὶ οἱ κατισχύοντες τοὺς λόγους μου ὡσεὶ τὰ ἄστρα τοῦ οὐρανοῦ εἰς τὸν αἰῶνα τοῦ αἰῶνος. 4 καὶ σύ, Δανιηλ, κάλυψον τὰ προστάγματα καὶ σφράγισαι τὸ βιβλίον ἕως καιροῦ συντελείας, ἕως ἂν ἀπομανῶσιν οἱ πολλοὶ καὶ πλησθῇ ἡ γῆ ἀδικίας. 5 καὶ εἶδον ἐγὼ Δανιηλ καὶ ἰδοὺ δύο ἕτεροι εἱστήκεισαν, εἷς ἔνθεν τοῦ ποταμοῦ καὶ εἷς ἔνθεν. 6 καὶ εἶπα τῷ ἑνὶ τῷ περιβεβλημένῳ τὰ βύσσινα τῷ ἐπάνω· Πότε οὖν συντέλεια ὧν εἴρηκάς μοι τῶν θαυμαστῶν καὶ ὁ καθαρισμὸς τούτων; 7 καὶ ἤκουσα τοῦ περιβεβλημένου τὰ βύσσινα, ὃς ἦν ἐπάνω τοῦ ὕδατος τοῦ ποταμοῦ· Ἕως καιροῦ συντελείας. καὶ ὕψωσε τὴν δεξιὰν καὶ τὴν ἀριστερὰν εἰς τὸν οὐρανὸν καὶ ὤμοσε τὸν ζῶντα εἰς τὸν αἰῶνα θεὸν ὅτι εἰς καιρὸν καὶ καιροὺς καὶ ἥμισυ καιροῦ ἡ συντέλεια χειρῶν ἀφέσεως λαοῦ ἁγίου, καὶ συντελεσθήσεται πάντα ταῦτα. 8 καὶ ἐγὼ ἤκουσα καὶ οὐ διενοήθην παρ᾽ αὐτὸν τὸν καιρὸν καὶ εἶπα· Κύριε, τίς ἡ λύσις τοῦ λόγου τούτου, καὶ τίνος αἱ παραβολαὶ αὗται; 9 καὶ εἶπέν μοι· Ἀπότρεχε, Δανιηλ, ὅτι κατακεκαλυμμένα καὶ ἐσφραγισμένα τὰ προστάγματα, ἕως ἂν 10 πειρασθῶσι καὶ ἁγιασθῶσι πολλοί, καὶ ἁμάρτωσιν οἱ ἁμαρτωλοί· καὶ οὐ μὴ διανοηθῶσι πάντες οἱ ἁμαρτωλοί, καὶ οἱ διανοούμενοι προσέξουσιν. 11 ἀφ᾽ οὗ ἂν ἀποσταθῇ ἡ θυσία διὰ παντὸς καὶ ἑτοιμασθῇ δοθῆναι τὸ βδέλυγμα τῆς ἐρημώσεως, ἡμέρας χιλίας διακοσίας ἐνενήκοντα. 12 μακάριος ὁ ἐμμένων καὶ συνάξει εἰς ἡμέρας χιλίας τριακοσίας τριάκοντα πέντε. 13 καὶ σὺ βάδισον ἀναπαύου· ἔτι γάρ εἰσιν ἡμέραι καὶ ὧραι εἰς ἀναπλήρωσιν συντελείας, καὶ ἀναπαύσῃ καὶ ἀναστήσῃ ἐπὶ τὴν δόξαν σου εἰς συντέλειαν ἡμερῶν.

12:1 "And in that time, Michael, the great prince who stands over the sons of your people, will stand, and it shall be a time of distress that has not happened since there was a nation until that time. And in that time, your people will escape – each one found written in the book. 2 And many will awake from the sleeping of the ground of dust: these to eternal life and these to disgrace and eternal loathing. 3 And the insightful will shine like the shining of the vault and those who cause righteousness for many as stars forever and ever. 4 But you, Daniel, stop up the words and seal the book until an end time. Many will roam, and knowledge will increase." 5 And I, Daniel, looked, and right there – two others were standing, one here at the bank of the river, and one here at the bank of the river. 6 And he said to the man clothed in linen who was over the waters of the river, "When is the end of the wonders?" 7 And I heard the man clothed in linen who was over the waters of the river, and he raised his right hand and his left to the heavens and swore by the one who lives forever that, "For a time, times, and a half. And when the shattering of the holy people's hand comes to an end, all these will come to an end." 8 And I heard, but I was not understanding. And I said, "My lord, what is after these?" 9 And he said, "Go, Daniel, because the words are stopped up and sealed until an end time. 10 Many will be purified, whitened, and refined, and the wicked will act wickedly and none of the wicked will understand. But the insightful will understand. 11 And from the time of the removing of the daily sacrifice and the setting of the desolated abomination is one thousand, two hundred, and ninety days. 12 Happy is the one who waits and reaches the one thousand, three hundred, and thirty-five days! 13 But you – go till the end, and you will rest. And you will stand at your lot at the end of days."